A WILLIAMSON W KIDS CAN!® BOOK

WORDPLAY

C · A · F · É

Cool Codes, Priceless Punzles® & Phantastic Phonetic Phun

Written & Illustrated by Michael Kline

Williamson Books • Nashville, Tennessee

Library of Congress Cataloging-in-Publication Data

Kline, Michael P.
 WordPlay café : cool codes, priceless punzles & phantastic phonetic phun / written and illustrated by Michael Kline.
   p. cm.
 "A Williamson kids can! book."
 Includes index.
 ISBN 0-8249-6753-4 (softcover)
 ISBN 0-8249-6773-9 (hardcover)
 1. Word games. I. Title.
 GV1507.W8K54 2005
 793.73'4—dc22
                                    2005002761

Kids Can! ® series editor: **Susan Williamson**
Project editor: **Emily Stetson**
Interior design: **Joseph Lee**
Illustrations: **Michael Kline**
Cover design and illustration: **Michael Kline**

Printed and bound in Italy by LEGO

Published by Williamson Books
An imprint of Ideals Publications
A division of Guideposts
535 Metroplex Drive, Suite 250
Nashville, Tennessee 37211
800-586-2572

10 9 8 7 6 5 4 3 2 1

A Note to the Afflicted

From the first emails to the last piece of this wordplay puzzle (this dedication), I've watched my friends and colleagues become infected with this verbal disease I have, the disease of wordplay. It's everywhere, affects everyone, and always leaves its victims changed (for the better!). Here are some casualties:

Many thanks to Susan Williamson, Kara Pekar, and especially Emily Stetson for their keen eyes and open minds, as well as their innate ability to make sense of this mess. My heart and medicine go out to my friend Joseph Lee for all he's put up with while designing this fabulous book (I owe you one, but you know that). To my boys, Steve and Jon, who rank among the top **Dominoes on Broadway** players on the planet and who inspire me constantly. And Baxter, I'll play with you in a minute if you'll just let me finish this. Last, but by far not least, to my wonderful wife, Vickie, who has the unenviable job of nodding in agreement and saying, "Yes, dear. That is very funny" whenever I chance to level another pun at her. I love you bunny.

Acknowledgments

The author wishes to thank the following for their contributions to WordPlay Café, whether through inspiration or careful notation: Will Shortz, Richard Lederer, Philip Furia, Bob Levey, Dave Morice, Anu Garg, Wiley Miller, and (posthumously) George Herriman.

Credits & permissions: page 19: "How Language Began: 5 Theories," *Kids Discover* (Vol. 10, Issue 3), www.kidsdiscover.com; pages 20 and 22: Permission is granted by Williamson Books to use language origin word roots previously published in *Ancient Greece!* and *Ancient Rome!*; page 23: American playwright George Bernard Shaw coined the term "ghoti fillets" to demonstrate the difficulty of the English language; page 29: Scrabble and Monopoly are registered trademarks of Hasbro, Inc.; page 32: "A man, a plan, a canal: Panama" was written by Leigh Mercer, and is considered by many authorities to be one of the finest palindromes ever written; page 36: Thanks to Sam Taggar and Susan Williamson for their rendition of this game in *Great Games!* (Williamson Books); pages 38-39: Balderdash is a registered trademark of Gameworks Creations, Inc.; page 42: "The Night Before Christmas" (or "Account of a Visit from St. Nicholas"); page 47: "Jabberwocky," from *Through the Looking-Glass, and What Alice Found There* by Lewis Carroll (London: Macmillan and Co., 1872); page 51: NON-SEQUITUR © 2003 Wiley Miller. Dist. By UNIVERSAL PRESS SYNDICATE. Reprinted with permission. All rights reserved.; *Krazy Kat* image, 1918 (public domain); page 78: "I Am the Very Model of a Modern Major-General," from Gilbert and Sullivan's operetta *The Pirates of Penzance*, which premiered December 31, 1879, in New York; page 99: *photigue* neologism contributed by Jennifer Lutz and published in the May 2000 online column (www.fun-with-words.com/neologisms_competition.html); page 119: Thanks to Amanda Hargis and her mnemonics website (Amanda's Mnemonics Page, http://users.frii.com/geomanda/mnemonics.html).

Contents

Contents (continued)

Chapter Fore

DEEP-FRIED DICTION FOR TWO (OR MORE!) 73

Chapter 5ive

PC PANCAKES: WORD GAMES WITH A COMPUTER 107

Chapter Sicks

PUT WORDS TO WORK IN YOUR KITCHEN 117

Resources

ARE YOU HUNGRY?

All of us at the WORDPLAY CAFÉ want to welcome you. Here you will find food of every kind: soups and stews, pastries and pies, cookies and casseroles. Sound familiar? You many think so, but wait! The meals we serve are *Food for the Brain!*

By now you're probably asking, "What is this guy talking about?" The answer is quite simple. There is an old proverb, or saying, that goes something like this: "If you give a person a fish, you will feed him for a day. But if you teach a person *how* to fish, you will feed

her for the rest of her life." And that is exactly what this book is about. You'll find no crossword puzzles here for you to fill in and no word searches to circle. In short, there should be no reason for you to take a pencil (or an eraser, for that matter) to this book anywhere.

A Menu for Me 'N' U

What you *will* find in this book are instructions, or "recipes," as I like to call them, that will show you not only

how to *play* word games but how to *make up* word games of your own as well. Yikes! Sound like school? Nah, don't worry. It's way more fun than that.

I will teach you games that you can play many different times, in many different ways, with many different words and with many friends for many years.

So if you're hungry and you want to have some fun (not to mention impress a few friends), just grab your oven mitts, dust off your soup ladle, and let's get cooking, at the WORDPLAY CAFÉ!

Who *is* This Guy?

Boy, that's a good question. Well, for starters, my name is Michael Kline and I've been illustrating Williamson books for about 10 years. Some of my "hyper-doodling" appears in *Kids Discover* magazine as well, a relationship that has spanned (so far) nearly 14 years.

I live and work in Wichita, Kansas, but largely because of the Internet, I am able to work with publishers all over the country. Pretty cool, eh? But why did I choose to write and illustrate a book on *wordplay*?

It's because I am a wordplay freak! There's really no other way to put it. I am fascinated by the way that words work, the way they *don't* work sometimes, the manner in which they fit together, their relationships with one another, and above all, the way they *sound!*

Wherever I go, whatever I'm doing — watching TV, playing dominoes with friends, or whatever — I am always listening. I'm listening for those times when words don't always do what they're supposed to do. And I am here (hear?) to encourage you to do the same.

Ear We Go!

I could go on and on about how important it is to have a good vocabulary, how invaluable good grammar is, or why you should know how to spell correctly. Teachers and parents could talk for days (and sometimes do!) on proper sentence structure and writing skills. But as far as wordplay goes, there is one thing you need more than anything else. This one thing (well, two, really) will guide you further into the world of noun-trouncing than you could ever imagine. Know what it is?

It's what keeps your glasses up, prevents your hat from falling down around your head, and gives you a place to hang your headphones. Of course, it's your ears!

What Did He Say?

Nearly every person who ever flung a phrase or penned a pun will tell you that the most important tool to have in your wordplay cupboard is a good set of ears. Why? Because most wordplay originates from listening to things that people say (and write). Just listen. Listen with your phonetic radar turned to HIGH! And if you hear (or read) something funny, write it down. With a little "kitchen" practice, you, too, can start to have a sense of how wordplay works and how much fun it can be.

Oh, and about my spelling: You may come across what appear at first glance to be misspelled words in this book.

Man does not live by bread alone. Tuna, however, is another story...

Trust me, no words that I use are accidents. If I spell something a little differently than you are used to seeing it, I have a good reason for doing so (even if that reason is "just for the fun of it").

Also, you need to know that I am not alone in this effort.

I am often in the company of my cat Baxter (okay, my wife's cat). He comes into my office on a regular basis, checks up on what I am doing, offers any advice that he feels is needed, then proceeds to stretch out in the closest patch of sunlight.

I think he does this to remind me of his consultation-only status. He is a cat and I am merely a human. At any rate, I have chosen to let him speak on a variety of subjects, as you will see.

The Rules You Do & Don't Need to Follow
(& other daily specials)

Whenever you go into a restaurant, there's usually a sign on the door that says something like No Shoes, No Shirt, No Service. Well, this is a rule, and there is a reason for it. Your local health department is trying to watch out for your safety and the safety of others.

Seeing as how the WORDPLAY CAFÉ is in the business of preparing food, we have some rules, too, as follows:

Never, never, ever use words that would cause anyone harm or that would make fun of someone. Words were invented to open communication between people, not to shut it down.

There is absolutely no place for foul language or swear words at the WORDPLAY CAFÉ, no matter what you might hear on the playground or on TV. People who use offensive language are doing so because they are not smart enough to get their points across any other way, so they are taking the easy way out and going for the "shock" value of a word. Don't you fall into that trap.

Ask questions! Whenever I visit schools and talk to kids about wordplay and art, I always try to sneak in a word that no one knows. After a few seconds, I ask someone what that word meant, and rarely does anyone have the correct answer. So I say, "Why didn't you stop me and ask what that word meant?" If there's ever anything you don't understand, take the time to ask the question.

Conjugate Two Verbs & Call Me in the Morning (a word or two on word indigestion)

We all use words. Whether we think them, say them, see them, or write them, words are a very important part of how we communicate.

We sing them and shout them, and sometimes actions speak louder than they do. Sometimes we're at a loss for them and they are beyond us. We have them with someone, and they stick in our mouths.

Every now and then we'll get them in edgewise, and sometimes we may even go back on them, but above everything else, we use them.

Take a Word from Me

My best friends know that I love words and wordplay. But I have one rule that I live by, over anything else:

Nobody is a bigger fool than I am.

I make mistakes all of the time. Screw up, mess up, goof up; whatever you want to call it, I'm usually in the middle of it. I never take things very seriously, and without fail, the first person I laugh at is *me!*

I would ask that as you experiment with playing with words as I have here at the WORDPLAY CAFÉ, keep my attitude in mind. It will be your choice to choose and use words in ways that are fun as well as expressive, but do so with care, keeping in mind the rules on page 7. If people around you know that you have only good intentions with wordplay, they'll join in, too!

Happy cooking!

Play with Your Food!

Okay, now that we've gone over the basic rules for the WORDPLAY CAFÉ, let's spend a few minutes on the rules that you *don't* have to follow.

When I talk about a game and how it is played, I am giving you guidelines as to how the game *could* be played. But honestly, most wordplay has come from people who ignore the rules and have extraordinary eyesight. You may see a better way to play the game or you may see how some words relate to others in ways not yet thought of.

Wordplay is a rather dynamic pastime, one that changes all the time. There are now many websites devoted to wordplay and word games, and people are always thinking up new ways to play with their words. I want to encourage you to do the same. Here at the WORDPLAY CAFÉ, we want you to *play with your food!*

Huh?

Is the author a few sandwiches short of a picnic? Did he just suggest playing with your food? You bet! Except in this case, your food is *words*. Twist words, turn them, flip them and flop them, rearrange them, and whip them into a frenzy! In short, look at words in ways you've never done before. If your words refuse to move, then move yourself, as in standing on your head, for instance.

Take a look at my recipes for each game, give them a try, and then perhaps be thinking about another way to play them. Who knows? In five or ten years, you may be writing your own book of wordplay recipes!

Which brings us to …

THE RECIPES

With most games at the WORDPLAY CAFÉ, you'll see a recipe that includes a list of ingredients and a short description on how the game is prepared. I'll also list how many each recipe "serves," plus how much skill is required, indicated by the oven temperature setting: LOW, MEDIUM, or HIGH.

Some recipes include CHEF'S TIPS for explaining variations or helpful pointers. If you can think of a better way to play, simply add your own ingredients, serving suggestions, and temperature setting.

understudy: why you get yelled at in school.

UNFORTUNATE COOKIES

These will pop up from time to time because I have just thought of a word that sounds like, or means, something else. Like fortune cookies, they dispense bits of "wisdom." Unfortunately, they are completely made up. UNFORTUNATE COOKIES are a perfect example of playing with your food. First I'll give the word, then my made-up definition.

If you can think of any UNFORTUNATE COOKIES, by all means write them down!

stopwatch: when a person stares at a red light.

Brain Candy

Every now and then I will ask you to stop and ponder a certain question, or I'll give you a definition for a word or term, or maybe I'll just relate some interesting word history. I call it BRAIN CANDY because it's food for thought, just in case your bucket of gray matter missed breakfast this morning!

BAXTER SAYS *WHAT?*

Actually, my cat Baxter never says anything except for *meow*, which can mean "I'm hungry," "I'm hungry," or "I'm hungry." But sometimes, just by the look in his eyes, I know he's trying to tell me other things. He is only a casual observer in my office, but his distance from anything that even resembles work gives him wisdom well beyond his actual height.

Occasionally, I will let him have his say in this book, because some of his insights make sense; that is, *if* I am translating them correctly.

Baxter Says:

What inspires you? When you have a lot of homework to do, is there a favorite place that you can work without being disturbed? Is there a favorite kind of music that you like to listen to?

Take the advice of someone who has worked at home (okay, watched my human work) for many years: When you have a lot of work to do, be nice to yourself. Find a comfortable, well-lit place (make sure all of the materials you need are within easy reach) with perhaps juice, milk, or some kind of refreshment nearby, and put on some good (not distracting) music. Then, dive into your work. Trust me, it will go much faster than you can imagine, and the results will be spectacular!

KEYWORD KABOBS

A lot of kids use the Internet to look up things for fun and for homework. Instead of giving you website addresses that often change over time, I'm giving you some keywords to use with a *search engine*. That's not a real engine, but rather a website or program that

KEYWORD KABOBS

heteronym, homograph, homonym, homophone

searches a database of information and reports the most meaningful results. See page 109 for more fun with search engines, plus some very important rules to follow when you add Internet ingredients!

Taste Test

All good chefs taste their food before giving it to someone else to eat, and for good reason! It's a way to check the flavor of something while it's on the stove. I'm going to ask you to check *my* cooking, too.

Look for the TASTE TEST icon every now and then with questions like "Can you find two palindromes in the poem on this page?" (You'll find the answers to these puzzlers printed on page 124, if you need them.)

NOODLE BOOK

What? A *Noodle Book*? Have birds been building a nest in the author's satellite dish? Quite likely (as my mom would say), but that's another book! I'd like you to consider finding and using some kind of journal, book, log, or diary to help you remember some of those fantastic word games you're going to come up with. I refer to mine as a NOODLE BOOK (noodle as in my "brain"), and I have several.

Why write your ideas down? If you're anything like me, you'll tend to forget things in five minutes, so a NOODLE BOOK helps to keep track of your thoughts. Maybe it will help to keep your noodle from roaming off (Noodles Romanoff!). And just for the fun of it, be sure to doodle in your NOODLE BOOK, too!

PUNZLES®?

As I mentioned earlier, it's a lot of fun to sit around and listen to the things people say. When I do, I listen for what people are saying *phonetically*. That is, when I hear someone use the word **chalkboard**, of course I know what is meant, but what I hear is **"chalk bored."** Then I ask myself, "Why is the chalk bored? Isn't there anything to do?"

Out of this unusual manner of listening to people, I began to create PUNZLES®, short for "pun puzzles." Instead of a pun being spoken or written out as a joke, I thought it would be more fun to draw a pun, and then let the viewer try to guess the familiar-sounding word or phrase that the image represents.

I began doing pun puzzles just for my own amusement, but when I showed them at schools, kids really got a kick out of them. So I began to draw them for magazines, and even turned a few into electronic greeting cards!

Try This!

To play PUNZLES® is simple. Just look at what's going on in the picture, start saying some keywords to yourself over and over, and after a while the phrase or word will come to you. If you need

PUNZLES®

help, you'll find the answer printed somewhere else, most likely upside down or backward (I don't want to make it *too* easy).

If you read the answer and groan, or if you show the PUNZLES® to someone else and they say, "Oh, that is *really* bad!", then congratulations! You've just stumbled on the number one reason to pun. In short, the best puns are usually the worst (or should I say "wurst"!).

Above all else, have *fun*! And remember to keep those ears open.

Chapter Won

WORD NUTRITION

TABLE NO.	DINERS	SERVING NO.	001

From Aardvark to Zoologist,
We find words everywhere,
In planes, on plains, and when it rains,
And even in our hair!

With alphabets and origins
And history to spare,
We'll sling some slang and fling a phrase,
So Know-it-Alls, beware!

Blue Plate Special

Words: A Brief History

(& not a story about underwear)

Words have been around for a long, long time. More than 5,000 years ago people in ancient Mesopotamia (where the Middle East is today) kept records by carving small symbols into flat, wet clay tablets. And the origins of *that* writing may go back thousands of years earlier, when people made different shapes and symbols on clay tokens to keep track of what they were trading.

Since then, humans have tried to communicate by carving symbols on bones and stones, by painting on leaves and *papyrus* (a material made by the ancient Egyptians from a water plant), by writing on paper, and eventually by typing words into a word processor and watching them magically appear on a computer screen, just as you do when you email your friends. Pretty cool, isn't it,

given all that history? (Whew! Writing really *is* an antediluvian art!)

Today there are about 5 billion people (around 85 percent of the earth's population) who can read and write. Are you one of those? Oh, I guess you are, or you wouldn't be reading this, would you?

I beg your pardon!

KEYWORD KABOBS

hieroglyph, ideograph, morpheme, paleography, phonemes, pictograph, runes, syllabary

Taste Test

Can you find a word on this page that means "ancient"? (Answer on page 124.)

26 Main Ingredients
(a.k.a. the alphabet)

Did you ever stop to think that every letter in the alphabet is actually like a little sign, telling you where to go, what to do next?

Each letter has its own specific place, its own sound, and its own special characteristics. Even though the typeface may change (**like this**), a letter has the same purpose: to make words.

Imagine having 26 very good friends. They will play with you as long as you want, they can produce hilarious results, and they never get tired. If you add 10 numbers to that equation (which is often handy), you have 36 great buddies. And hey, let's not leave out the punctuation pals! They can be a great source of inspiration and fun, too.

You may be surprised to learn that most pocket dictionaries list more than 40,000 words, and some of the scholarly dictionaries boast over 470,000! And those are just the English language dictionaries. You can't tell me that there's nothing to do with that many possibilities!

Check out LICENSE PL8 PIE (page 62), PORTRAIT PICKLES (page 66), and INITIAL INGREDIENTS (page 81), for more alphabet fun.

The word *nitpicker* originally meant someone who picked the tiny eggs of lice (nits) from someone's hair! Today, it is used to describe someone who looks for and finds small errors! Are you a nitpicker?

Why Words?

This may sound like a no-brainer, but have you ever tried to buy a movie ticket without using words? How about answering a question? It may be easy for the yes and no answers, but try to give three examples of a chemical reaction or explain different kinds of clouds, without the use of words.

Let's face it, words are very important to know! In many cultures, your overall intelligence is based largely on the number of words in your vocabulary. I hate to nitpick here, but how many words do you suppose are in *your* vocabulary? If you really want to know, begin with the letter A and write down all the A words you can think of while your friends do the same. (No fair just adding an S or adding ING or similar endings. Each word has to be different!) Then count 'em up and see who makes the A-List!

Signed, Sealed, and Delivered

Even people without the ability to speak or to hear have a large vocabulary. American Sign Language (ASL) is a visual-spatial language of the deaf or hearing impaired that consists of not only the 26 letters of the alphabet, but more than 1,200 unique terms as well. Signing Exact English (SEE), which is closer to the actual English language, has more than 4,520 different illustrations, with a total word potential of about 60,000 words!

When people who can hear trade words, they use *inflections*, or stresses on a certain syllable of a word. The hearing impaired also stress certain words or phrases, by raising or furrowing their eyebrows.

KEYWORD KABOBS

ASL, body language, gesticulation, kinesics, mime, pantomime, sign language

Wordless Waffles

Some people tend to take the ability to speak for granted, especially those who shout or use four-letter words (a no-no, as I know *you* know). But you can whip up something fun and delicious without using any words at all!

Recipe

serves: 2 or more players

ingredients:

- Pencil and paper

skill level
LOW · MEDIUM · HIGH

Let's Cook!

Make a list of 10 common phrases that you would use on a daily basis, such as *What time will dinner be ready?* or *Do I have to go to school?* or perhaps *I'm all done with my homework. Can I go out and play?* Ask an adult to be the judge, and then take turns trying to convey your message to another person without speaking or writing. You can use your hands or facial expressions, point to objects, do anything except make noise.

Keep track of who "wins" the most phrases. You can even award a Charlie Chaplin Award, named for the famous actor in silent movies, to the best WORDLESS WAFFLES act!

decline: de person dat draws de pictures in dis book.

Word Power Pizza

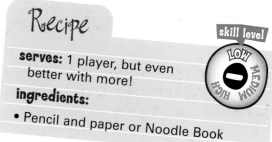
Forget that playground chant "Sticks and stones will break my bones, but words can never hurt me." Words can be very powerful things! The entire country of the United States (as well as many others) has operated for many years based on words — the Constitution, the Bill of Rights, the Declaration of Independence, to name a few. Words have brought comfort and laughter to many people, too. Words have even made some people famous forever. But, yes, words can leave a real sting. People have had their feelings hurt, have gone to prison, and have suffered terribly, all because of words they used or words others used against them. Words have built nations and destroyed them. Wars have even begun over words.

Today, many companies operate around what is called a *mission statement*, which is simply the principles, purposes, and objectives of the organization that are written down. Putting the ideas in writing, with words, helps everyone involved better understand what the organization hopes to accomplish. Isn't it amazing how individual words, when put together, can be so powerful?

Let's Cook!

Create a mission statement, or a personal Bill of Rights. Think about how you think things should be, not only for yourself, but for friends and family members as well. Or try writing one for a club you belong to. Make your WORD POWER PIZZA a group effort, just the way every slice of pizza contributes to make a whole pizza pie!

We, the kids of the Johnson household...

pungent: a man who enjoys wordplay.

Slanguage Slaw

Clown around, carry on, horse around, mess around, let loose, kick up your heels, cut up, strut your stuff, ham it up, whoop it up, and go on a tear!

Notice anything familiar? All of these phrases are perfectly acceptable slang for the word **play**. Slang (or slanguage) is a language that is often used in casual or playful speech in place of regular words, usually to achieve a special effect.

When I was younger, my mom had the thankless job of driving me everywhere (sound familiar?). I was always in a hurry, but instead of just asking my mom to drive a little faster, I would use slang such as "Put the pedal to the metal, Mom!" or "Shake a leg, Mom!" or "Drop the hammer, Mom!"

Am i There Yet?

Of course, none of these verbal encouragements ever got me anywhere any faster. They *did* get me stern looks from my mother, though. So if you choose to use slang, use it wisely!

It may take some time to recognize slang, but when you get used to picking it out, you'll start to hear it everywhere!

Then I got some big air, popped a 360, and almost bailed!

Bonus!

The next time you plop down (there's *one!*) in front of the TV, keep your fingers at the ready (there's *another!*) and start to jot down or count all of the slang terms you hear. Perhaps you and a friend can have a contest to see who is able to catch the most slang. Are you diggin' my noise?

cockney, colloquialism, jargon, jive, lingo, neologism, patois, pidgin, reduplicatives, slanguage, valspeak, vernacular

Ebonics, short for Ebony Phonics, is a dialect that has gotten some attention lately. It is also known as African American Vernacular English (AAVE) and is being heard more and more on street corners and at schools. Should Ebonics be allowed in the classroom, or even be taught as another language (like French or Spanish), or is it just another form of slang?

Can you find a seven-letter portmanteau (page 21) on this page that starts with E? Then, can you find another? (Answers on page 124.)

How Language Began: Five Theories

Many *linguists* (people who study languages) have a hard time agreeing on just how words and speech began. The fact that human language came about so long ago (some say more than 8,000 years ago) will likely prevent us from ever knowing.

In the early 1900s, linguist Otto Jespersen described four popular theories as to how human language began, and added his own theory (pooh-pooh) to make a fifth.

DING-DONG
According to the ding-dong theory, the first words came from people's reactions to the environment. For example, it has been suggested that "mama" reflects the movement of babies' lips as they get ready to nurse.

BOW-WOW
The bow-wow theory suggests that language arose from people imitating sounds of nature, especially animal calls.

YO-HE-HO
The yo-he-ho theory says that the first language came from people's need to work together, producing first grunts, then chants, then words.

LA-LA
The la-la theory supposes that the first sounds were associated with love, play, poetry, and song.

POOH-POOH
The pooh-pooh theory says that the first speech came from humans expressing emotions such as pain, anger, and frustration.

Orange Origin Juice

It might surprise you to learn that a lot of the words we use today have Latin and Greek origins. For example, the word **music** is from the Greek *Muses*, who were the daughters of Zeus, a god who represented the human arts. And the word **primate** is from the Latin *primus*, meaning "first."

In fact, you probably know more Greek and Latin than you think! If you breathe air and get ideas, you're using some words that come from Greek roots. **Air** comes from the Greek word *aer*, and **idea** has the Greek root word *idein*, meaning "to see." And even if you've never studied Latin, you probably speak it already! About 40 percent of English words have Latin roots. Recognize any of these?

do, color, condo, quiet, honor, multi, sane, insane, ridiculous, rare, unique, accuse, apparatus, pauper, furor, farina

bulky: what a bull uses to open the door.

They are all so-called English words that are actually Latin!

What's in a Name?

Scientists still use Latin names to identify the species of plants and animals on earth. That way, people all over the world can recognize and agree on the name of the species. These scientific names are usually in two parts, such as *Eleutherodactylus augusti* ("barking frog"). The first Latin word is the generic, or *genus*, name and the second is the specific, or *species*, name. You may already know your scientific name, *Homo sapiens*, meaning "wise man." Now, you try it!

Let's Cook!

Go around to the different rooms of your house and have each person write

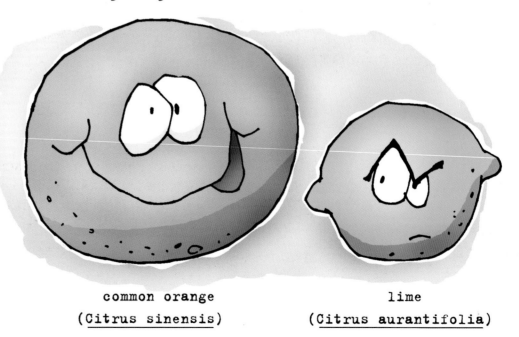

Orange you glad you asked?

common orange
(Citrus sinensis)

lime
(Citrus aurantifolia)

Timeorus
wastercanus

A *portmanteau* (or "suit-case" word) is made from combining two words to form one, such as **brunch** (**br**eakfast and **lunch**), **motel** (**mot**or and ho**tel**), or **smog** (**smo**ke and fo**g**). Think of other portmanteaus or make up some of your own and play PORTMANTEAU the next time you are bored in the car or on the bus.

PUNZLES®

Trapezoid:
$A = (h(a + b))/2$,
in which h is the height,
a the longer parallel side,
and b the shorter.

Recipe

skill level

MEDIUM
LOW · HIGH
1

serves: 2 or more players

ingredients:

• Pencil and paper or Noodle Book

• 1 house or apartment

a Latin-sounding name for that room. Trade notes and see if your friends can decipher which room is being described from its "scientific name." Maybe I can start you off with the following: *Siblingus uncleanicus.*

Play Greektionary

Ancient Greek root and stem words can grow a whole tree of modern-day English words. Check out the list here. See any familiar words about to take root? How about *bio* + *logy* = "the study of life," as in **biology**? Or, *tele* + *phon* = "to speak far," as in **telephone**. What about the English word **acrobat**? See how many words (branches) you can make for your tree using a single Greek word root. Which word builds the biggest tree?

acro (highest)
agra (farm)
anthro (human)
arch (chief)
aristo (best)
astro (star)
audio (hearing)
auto (self)
batos (to go)
bio (life)
chromo (color)
chrono (time)
cosmos (world)
cracy (rule by)
demo (people)
graph (write)
hydro (water)
iso (equal)

ist (one who does something, like bicycl**ist**)
meter, metron (to measure)
micro (small)
mono (one)
nomy (rules for, management of, laws of)
ophy (wisdom about, knowledge of)
optikos (see)
philo (love)
phon (speak)
psyche (soul)
techne (skill, art)
tele (far)

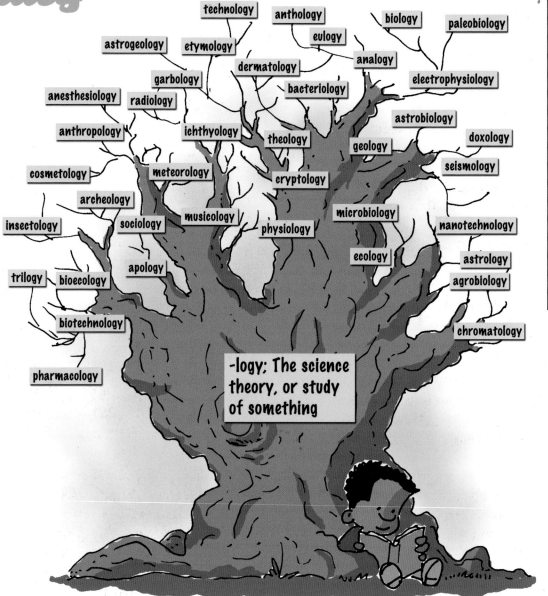

-logy: The science theory, or study of something

probate: something that only professional fishermen use.

Panfried Problems
(ghoti fillets)

Take several pieces of freshwater ghoti fillets and … Wait a minute: What are *ghoti fillets*? Perhaps if I helped you sound out the word, you'll understand where I'm headed.

Let's break it up into syllable sounds: "gh" as in **rough**, "o" as in **women**, and "ti" as in **nation**. See the problem?

As elegant and civil as we may think the English language is, it is full of problems, especially for people who learn English as a second language.

Part of the problem is that one symbol can be pronounced many ways. Take the letter A, for example. It can be used in the words **plate**, **fact**, or **instead**, all producing different sounds.

If that weren't bad enough, we use different spellings to make the same sound, as in the "a" sound in **rate**, in **main**, or in **weigh**.

Where Y'all From?

On top of all that, we have differences in our *dialects!* Depending on which part of the country you're from, you may choose to drink a **soda**, a **soft drink**, or a **pop**.

Could you bring me a soda, Pop?

What's more, there are also problems that come up when people translate one language into another. There are some words in English that don't even exist in other languages! (Check out TRANSLATION TOAST on page 112 to have some fun with that.)

Brain Candy

New words are always being invented. Do you suppose your grandparents ever used the word **email**, or the acronym **VCR**? Can you think of other recent additions to our language? Imagine Lewis telling Clark that he wasn't able to "**log on**." What would that have meant?

I can't seem to log on.

I think you're barking up the wrong tree.

parables: two large male bovines.

Spelling Bee Brownies (or what the buzz is all about)

Every year, kids from around the country test their spelling skills in the Scripps National Spelling Bee, held in Washington, D.C. They begin at their local schools or community bees and progress until just over 250 contestants make it to the finals.

The spelling bee was begun by a newspaper, the Louisville (Kentucky) *Courier-Journal* in 1925. The Scripps Howard News Service took over the spelling bee in 1941. The bee has grown from 9 original contestants to 265 finalists in 2004.

The contest is limited to kids in the eighth grade or under the age of 16 at the date of the final competition.

A Bee in Her Bonnet

Here's something worth noting: Out of 80 past champions, 38 were boys and 42 were girls. There was no bee held in the years 1943, 1944, and 1945 because of World War II, and in the years 1950, 1957, and 1962, there were co-champions (two winners).

If you think you're a word wizard and want to give it a try, ask your teacher or local home-schooling organization for more details, or check out the spelling bee information yourself at www.spellingbee.com.

apiary.
A-P-I-A-R-Y.
apiary.

nectar.
N-E-C-T-A-R.
nectar.

punt: what you are when someone hits you with a pun.

Recipe

serves: 2 or more players (if you have lots of kids, make teams of 4 or 5 contestants each)

ingredients:
- Pencil and paper
- Dictionary
- 1 or more adults
- Timer or watch

Let's Cook!

Organize your own spelling bee. Ask a parent or other adult to serve as Pronouncer (and Judge). Have that person prepare a list of unusual (but not *terribly* difficult) words from the dictionary.

The play goes in rounds, with each team getting the same number of words. The Pronouncer states the word to the Speller, who gets two minutes to repeat the word, spell the word, and then repeat the word again. The Speller may ask the Pronouncer to say the word again, define it, or use it in a sentence. If the Speller misspells the word, the same word goes to the competing player (or other team). Each correctly spelled word gets a point. Here's an example to get you going:

> **Pronouncer:** *Persnickety.*
> **Speller:** *Could you give me the word in a sentence, please?*
> **Pronouncer:** *The persnickety English teacher accepted only typed, not hand-written, homework.*
> **Speller:** *Persnickety. P-E-R-S-N-I-C-K-E-T-Y. Persnickety.*

Maybe you could have a tray of brownies as the grand prize!

jambalaya.
J-A-M-B-A-L-A-Y-A
jambalaya.

number: an anesthesiologist. (Look it up!)

Taste Test ❓❓❓

Don't feel bad if you have a problem finding the right words.

Vice president Dan Quayle seemed to have an unusually difficult time when it came to using the correct words during the Bush administration of 1989–1993. Oftentimes he would struggle to find the proper words, with hilarious results. Here are just a few of his supposed blunders. See if you can find the mistakes, by reading every word he said, not what you know he meant to say. *To check your answers, turn to page 124.*

- This president is going to lead us out of this recovery. It will happen.
- When asked about Latin America: The U.S. has a vital interest in that area of the country.
- It's wonderful to be here in the great state of Chicago.
- I love California; I practically grew up in Phoenix.
- We are ready for any unforeseen event that may or may not occur.
- My friends, no matter how tough the road may be, we can and we will never, never surrender to what is right.
- A low voter turnout is an indication of fewer people going to the polls.
- If you give a person a fish, they fish for a day. But if you train a person to fish, they fish for a lifetime.
- We're going to have the best-educated American people in the world.
- It isn't pollution that's harming our environment. It's impurities in our air and water that are doing it.

PUNZLES®

It's wonderful to be here in the great state of Chicago.

KEYWORD KABOBS

Quayleisms

Chapter Too

COMFORT FOOD: A BITE OF TRADITIONAL WORD GAMES

TABLE NO.	DINERS	SERVING NO.	002

They've been around for many years,
Those games your grandma plays,
Like palindromes and anagrams
And Scrabble (just a craze?)

So don't be square, just hang in there
And we will show you how
To cook your words and slice your verbs
And when to take a bow.

Wall-Nut Words

There's a pretty good chance that if you know any words at all (and obviously you know a bunch!), you've tried your hand at crossword puzzles, which can be found in just about any newspaper. There are also cryptograms, word crosses, word searches, word squares, logic problems, word jumbles, and all kinds of other word games.

One of the most popular word games ever invented is Scrabble, in which you take wooden tiles of individual letters and build words across or down on a board.

Would you like to learn a similar game (oops, *recipe*) that is much more vertical? If your mom ever caught you drawing on the wall when you were younger, you'll appreciate this version, and it's not nearly as dangerous!

Recipe

skill level

serves: 2 or more players

ingredients:

• Pencil

• Pad of self-stick notes, such as Post-it Notes (I like to use the real sticky kind)

Let's Cook!

Write a letter on each note until you've completed the alphabet as shown. For the more common letters, you'll need several copies. While you're writing the letter, add a "point" number to the corner of each note to score with.

Turn each sticky note over so you can't see the letter, and spread them all out on a table. To play, each player picks up seven notes, and, in turn, builds a word on the wall, adding to any previously posted words. Keep score by counting up the points for each turn. When all the letters have been used, the player with the highest score wins!

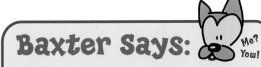

M E O W = 22 points

Baxter Says:

Me? Yow!

"Necessity is the mother of invention." If you can see a better or more fun way to play a game, you may be on your way to inventing a game that could turn out to be even more popular than Scrabble! Feel free to begin right now by changing the recipes for games you find here.

CHEF'S TIPS
• Each player should have seven letters to play with each time. So, if a player makes a word using four letters, she then picks up four more notes from the pile for her next turn.

Letter	How Many Needed	Points
A	10	1
B	2	10
C	2	10
D	5	5
E	10	1
F	2	10
G	4	10
H	2	10
I	8	1
J	2	10
K	2	10
L	5	5
M	2	10
N	5	5
O	8	1
P	2	10
Q	1	25
R	5	5
S	5	5
T	5	5
U	2	10
V	2	10
W	2	10
X	1	25
Y	2	10
Z	1	25

• Count the score on all the letters for each word you make, as in Scrabble (and not just the new letters you added).

Brain Candy

In the 1930s, Alfred Butts took his passion for crosswords and anagrams, and created a game he called Criss Cross Words as a personal pastime for family and friends. Game manufacturers of the time refused to market and produce his unique game, but in 1948 James Brunot and his wife (both avid Criss Cross Words players) felt they could make it work.

After several years of marketing and producing the game from a small shop in Dodgingtown, Connecticut, the Brunots began to realize their fortune in 1952, when orders began pouring in for the game. Today, Scrabble is owned by Hasbro, Inc. and ranks as the second best-selling game in America, just below Monopoly!

Add a Gram of Anagrams

Ever wonder what ingredients are in something as simple as, let's say, your name? Perhaps I can help separate and rearrange some of those ingredients for you.

An *anagram* is a word, phrase, or sentence that's made by rearranging the letters of another word, phrase, or sentence, often with hilarious results.

ANAGRAMS = AN ARM GAS
FUNERAL = REAL FUN
MATHEMATICS = TEACH SAM TIM
WORDPLAY CAFE = ROWDY PAL FACE
DEBIT CARD = BAD CREDIT
MICHAEL KLINE = MAN LIKE CHILE

See what I mean? It may seem difficult at first, but once you start to play with anagrams, you'll see anagrams in almost every word you use. I do, and I love it (even when it begins to take over my life!).

Brain Candy

There are many different kinds of anagrams. The most clever are those where the first word or phrase relates to the second, as in **FRIED** = **FIRED**, or **KITCHEN** = **THICKEN**. There is even an anagram equation! How about **TWELVE** + **ONE** = **ELEVEN** + **TWO**?

First period.

Or fried spit.

building: what a duck gets when it runs into something with its bill.

PUNZLES®

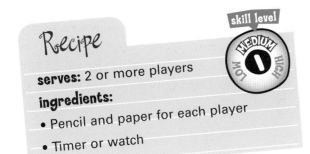

Recipe

skill level

MEDIUM

serves: 2 or more players

ingredients:

• Pencil and paper for each player

• Timer or watch

Let's Cook!

Choose the title of a current movie, song, or the name of your favorite book — something with a name that isn't too short — and give the players five minutes to come up with as many anagrams as they can. Remember, you need to use *all* the letters in order for it to be a true anagram.

CHEF'S TIPS *To see all the possibilities for anagrams more quickly, write all the letters in a circle, as I've done with* **dormitory**. *That way, the letters are scrambled and new words show up more easily.*

Taste Test ???

The word **dormitory** is an anagram of a two-word place that you likely know quite well. Can you figure out what it is? (Answer on page 124.)

Palindrome Potluck

What's a *palindrome*? Well, it's not about a friend who's just finished reading a novel about Italy's famous capital (Pal end *Rome*). Rather, it's a phrase or sentence that reads the same forward and backward. Here are a few to get you started:

A Toyota.
Tod sees Dot.
A man, a plan, a canal: Panama!
Draw, O coward!
Step on no pets.

Make up some of your own. Just pay attention to all the words used in everyday language, because you'll be surprised. And don't always look at whole words. The parts of words can provide some great fun, too (**Dr. Awkward**)! If it's easier, start with single words that are palindromes, like **civic**, **radar**, or **level**, then move on to phrases and even complete sentences.

Done with the newspaper yet, Dad?

Try This!

Ask an adult for the daily newspaper (he'll be shocked just to hear that) and start to read through it, making notes of how many palindromes you can find. Don't rule out the advertisements, either! If it's easier, look for simpler palindromes first, like **mom** and **pop** (even **dad** is one). Palindromes get easier all of a sudden, so keep at it. Before you know it, you'll start seeing them everywhere!

aibohphobia, palindromes, Sotades

apricot: something you can sleep on during the 4th month of the year.

A nut for a jar of tuna.

Brain Candy

Palindromes take their name from the Greek *palindromos*, which means "running back again." Isn't that a great name? They were the invention of Sotades of Maronia in the third century B.C. (some 2,300 or so years ago), who used them in clever ways to criticize the government. It is believed that ruler Ptolemy II was so angered by the palindromes that he had Sotades sealed up in a chest of lead and thrown into the sea. Let's hope that none of your palindromes have that effect on people!

Recipe

skill level: MEDIUM

serves: 2 players, but even greater fun with more!

ingredients:

- Pen or pencils and paper for each player
- Newspaper (with permission)
- Timer or watch

Let's Cook!

Hand a page of the newspaper to a friend or two, along with a pen or pencil for highlighting. Set the timer for five minutes, and see who comes up with the most palindromes.

Taste Test

Can you find two palindromes in the following poem?

Choosing sides with Steven
Was a daunting deed.
Never odd or even,
"Just decide!" I'd plead.

(Answer on page 124.)

Acrostic Appetizers

As I sit writing this book,
Cats play in the yard
Right under my window.
Often they seem to jump and
Spin, and when they
Think no one's looking, they
Inch their way up the bird feeder,
Causing all kinds of commotion.

Notice anything funny about the previous poem, other than the fact that the cats are playing rather than sleeping?

Check this out. Take the first letter of each line of the paragraph, and what do you get? That's right! A-C-R-O-S-T-I-C.

Acrostics are often (but not always) written as poems, with the initial letters being thought out in advance. Some acrostics are even related to the initial word as well, as in this example:

Fried rice and figs
Oats and okra
Ovens and olives
Dips and dumplings

The acrostic doesn't always have to be the first letters, though. Try one using the *last* letters in a paragraph or poem, as in:

"Please follow the path,"
Advised my dear ma,
"And then take a bath."
I countered, "Ha Ha!"

See how easy it is? Share the fun of acrostics. Here's the recipe.

Recipe

serves: 1 player and 1 pen pal
ingredients:
- Pencil and paper
- Stamp and envelope (or email)

skill level LOW MEDIUM HIGH

Let's Cook!

Write a birthday card or note to a friend using her first and last name, or the name of her pet or favorite activity, as an *acrostic*. (You might need to include a note with the definition of acrostic, just in case she doesn't get it!) If you email your note, keep in mind that an email may tend to *wrap* the text differently. You'll be amazed at how creative you can get!

Baxter Says:
Me? Yow!

Acrostics make wonderful handmade greeting (and get well) cards, and there's no better way to show someone you care than to spend some time on a friend. You will be repaid!

Word Lightning Lemonade

A re you as fast as lightning? Here's a recipe for a shocking game that can be played almost anywhere. I used to play this as a kid while waiting for all of my lemonade customers to come by. It involves seeing just how many words you know that begin with a certain letter. So, find a spot on the sidewalk and get your lemonade fixings!

Recipe

skill level

serves: 2 or more players

ingredients:
- Watch or timer

Let's Cook!

One player chooses a letter for everyone to use and calls it out. Each player in turn has one minute to call out as many words as he can think of that begin with that letter. (No repeats allowed!) The player with the most words wins the round. Then the next player picks a letter for everyone to use, and the game goes on.

H!

LEMONADE

Umm...
house, health,
horse, hear,
him, her,
umm... Help!

CHEF'S TIPS
- *To "bump up" the level of difficulty, have players use categories, such as names of fish, kids' first names, hobbies, whatever. For example, the first player might say, "Girls' names beginning with L."*
- *Give one person the job of timing and counting the words used.*
- *If you're playing with pencil and paper, set the timer and have players write down all the words they can think of for that letter at the same time. Then, compare your lists to see who has the most words (remember, only real words count!).*
- *Play A My Name Is Alice (see next page).*

paralyze: when you tell two fibs in a row.

A My Name is Alice

Using the alphabet poem below, take a turn going as far through the alphabet as you can. If you miss or hesitate, you lose your turn. You can play that you get to continue from where you stopped on your next turn or that you must start from the beginning of the alphabet again. The winner is the first person to get through the whole alphabet, or the player who gets furthest. Clap the rhythm of the alphabet words for even more fun!

A my name is ALICE, my husband's name is AL,
We live in ALABAMA and we sell APPLES.

B my name is BOBBY, my wife's name is BARB,
We live in BERMUDA and we sell BUGS.

C my name is CAROL, my husband's name is CARL,
We live in COLORADO and we sell CRABS.

(Got the idea? You take it from here!)

safety: tea that's okay to drink.

Baxter Says: Me? Yow!

"When life hands you lemons, make lemonade!" What's the difference between a lemon and lemonade? Sugar! So, this saying means that you should try to find the positive side of every situation.

Brain Candy

Have you ever heard someone refer to a car as a "lemon"? That's because — without something to sweeten it — lemons and lemonade can be quite bitter to swallow, as can knowing that you have a car that always breaks down!

Hangman Hash

One of the simplest and most popular games ever played is also one of the most gruesome. Anyone who has ever played Hangman knows that losing can seem rather — er — final.

Let's Cook!

First, determine the category (such as famous actress, or names of cars). Strike an underline for each letter used, leaving spaces where needed. Next, draw your gallows. Play usually goes pretty quick, so all of you Michelangelos out there (like myself) may find your friends telling you to "hurry up!"

As a player guesses a letter, a space is filled in or a body part is added until the player can either correctly identify the word(s), or is, well … let's just say that the player gets a little taller. Hmmm?

We always played by adding a head, body, left arm, right arm, left leg, right leg, and finally a noose. If you'd like to make it easier, use extra body parts like hair, hands, or feet. Just be sure to agree on the number of parts before the game starts. Some players even count the parts of the gallows as a guess.

Draw this part first

then these parts for the hangman

Spaces for letters go down here

Don't be discouraged if you don't do well at first. When I used to play with my kids, I lost so many times that they would refer to me as "Swing Daddy"! (Very funny…)

Recipe

serves: 2 players
ingredients:
• Pencil and paper

skill level

Brain Candy

Were you ever told to "hang in there"? This American phrase was originally used in the sport of boxing by managers who urged their fighters to stay in the game or "refuse to give up," even if it meant hanging onto the ropes.

CHEF'S TIPS *If you want to save yourself some paper, cut the body parts and parts for the gallows from self-stick notes, and stick your hangman game on the wall.*

Add a Dash of Balderdash!

Balderdash (and a board game of the same name) is one of the most fun games ever played, especially with a group of people. And what makes it even funnier is how it benefits the person who's the best fibber.

Sprinkle a little balderdash at your next birthday party or family get-together, and see what kind of fun you can easily cook up.

Let's Cook!

One player is chosen to be the Reader. She finds a word in the dictionary that she believes no one will know, reads the word aloud, then secretly writes down its true definition. The other players each write down a plausible-sounding definition of their own. The Reader then collects the definitions, mixes in the true one from the dictionary, and reads them all aloud in a natural voice.

The other players close their eyes, and as the Reader carefully reads the

Recipe

skill level
LOW MEDIUM HIGH

serves: 3 or 4 or more!

ingredients:
- Dictionary
- Pencils and several pieces of paper

zephyr: a small marsupial from Australia

zephyr: to join two pieces of hardwood

bulldoze: when a bull takes a short nap.

definitions one more time, each player "votes" by raising her hand for the definition she feels is correct.

Players get one point for each vote for their "incorrect" definition. If no one guesses the correct definition, the Reader gets three points. If a player guesses the correct definition, that person gets two points, and becomes the next Reader.

The more likely your definition, the more likely you'll fool the others!

zephyr: a west wind

zephyr: one who mixes peanut butter and pickles with tofu and spinach

Brain Candy

Balderdash! Sounds like someone cussing, doesn't it? Actually, no one knows the real origin of the word. It first turned up in the late 1500s and meant a type of drink. It would later come to be known as a mixed-up type of drink, which is probably where the game got its name from.

Word Square Snack

People (young and old) have been snacking on word square games for many years. They were popular even before crossword puzzles were invented.

To play this game, you need a strategy. But be forewarned; sometimes even the best strategy will not pay off! And just like piano lessons (yikes!), the more you play, the better you become.

Recipe

skill level: MEDIUM

serves: 2 or more players

ingredients:

• Pencil and several pieces of paper

• Lots of chewing on your tongue and saying "Hmmm..."

KEYWORD KABOBS

crossword puzzles,
sator square, tic tac toe,
word squares

Let's Cook!

Each person makes a 5-square by 5-square grid on her paper (a total of 25 small squares). Each player, in turn, calls out one letter that all players write wherever they want, as many times as they like, on their grids (this is part of the strategy). Players continue calling out different letters until all the squares in the grid are filled. The player with the most points for her words wins.

start out something like this...

```
        c
  b   a   b   y
  a   r
  h
```

CHEF'S TIPS

• *Words need to be at least three letters long.*

• *Words can go horizontally, vertically, or diagonally. Some games allow backward words, too. (Always agree on what exactly your rules are before you begin to play.)*

• *Award one point for each letter of each complete word (so a five-letter word would receive five points). You could also reward the Einsteins in the group who manage five-letter words by giving them 10 or even 20 points.*

• *Just for the fun of it, the losers get to make macaroni and cheese for the winner!*

Baxter Says:

Me? Yow!

Games involving wordplay have been around much longer than videos, television, and radio, yet we still play them. Does this tell you anything?

Chapter Free

DINNER FOR ONE: SINGLE-SERVING SYLLABLE SILLINESS

TABLE NO.	DINERS	SERVING NO.	003

Now on we go to headlines bad
As homonyms abound,
Reflect on words we think we know,
Then take it underground!

We'll zeugma verbs and dash off codes
And pickle all our friends.
imagination is the key—
& fun? it nevR Nds!

Homonym Grits

'Twas the knight before Christmas,
End awl threw the house,
Knot a creature was stirring,
Knot even a mouse.

How many misspelled words can you find in these first four lines of the famous poem "The Night Before Christmas"?

How about *none*?

That's right, my fellow phrase flingers, there are *no* misspelled words. There is, however, some terrible word usage.

All of the words that seem out of place are actually *homonyms* (also called *homophones*), words that sound alike (and are sometimes even spelled alike) but have different meanings.

Here's another example: The word **bear** can mean "to carry a heavy load," but it can also mean the animal, and the word **bare** is usually what babies are.

If yew give it sum thought and keep yore ears open, yule find their are mini different homonyms that people yews awn a daily bases.

Recipe

skill level MEDIUM (LOW · HIGH)

serves: 1 or more players

ingredients:

- Pencil and paper or Noodle Book

- A famous poem, nursery rhyme, or song (or even a passage from the Bible or the Declaration of Independence!)

—KEYWORD— KABOBS

___

heteronym, homograph,
homonym, homophone

The aunts go marching won bye won, hurrah, hurrah

The aunts go marching won bye won, hurrah, hurrah

The aunts go marching won bye won,

The little won stops too suck his thumb

And they awl go marching down too the ground

Two get out of the reign, BOOM! BOOM! BOOM!

The aunts go marching too bye to, hurrah, hurrah

The aunts go marching two bye to, hurrah, hurrah

The aunts go marching too bye too,

The little won stops too tye his shoo

And they awl go marching down two the ground

Two get out of the reign, BOOM! BOOM! BOOM!

incline: for the moment at least, Cheetohs, a ham sandwich, and a Dr. Pepper.

Let's Cook!

Take the passage of your choosing and rewrite it using homonyms.

Ask someone else to read what you've written and check it for misspelled words. Imagine her surprise when you reveal the secret!

CHEF'S TIPS *If you have trouble with a certain word, keep saying it slowly over and over until you figure out if the word is a homonym of some other word.*

Taste Test

How many homonyms (and close-sounding words) can you find used in an incorrect way in the text on pages 42 and 43? A hint: There are at least 16! (Answers on page 124.)

The aunts go marching three bye three, hurrah, hurrah

The aunts go marching three bye three, hurrah, hurrah

The aunts go marching three bye three,

The little won stops too climb uh tree

And they awl go marching down too the ground

Two get out of the reign, BOOM! BOOM! BOOM!

The aunts go marching fore bye fore, hurrah, hurrah

The aunts go marching fore bye fore, hurrah, hurrah

The aunts go marching fore bye fore,

The little won stops too shut the door

And they awl go marching down too the ground

Two get out of the reign, BOOM! BOOM! BOOM!

Homophone means "same sound" in Greek. Homonyms are responsible for many popular *puns*, or words or expressions that use different ideas in a humorous way, as in the following joke:

A Shetland pony walks into a convenience store and says, "I'd like to buy a candy bar." The clerk looks at him and says, "I can hardly hear you." The pony says, "I'm sorry, but I'm just a little hoarse."

Get it? See pages 74 to 77 for more homonym and pun fun.

Verbal Tea (& other code remedies)

Did I hear you say you had a *bad code*? Having trouble saying your words clearly? Perhaps some *nouns* are caught in your throat or your *adjectives* are running? Well, we have just the remedy!

Codes have been around for a long time and have served many useful purposes. Archaeologists who study ancient Egyptian or Central American *hieroglyphs* (writing that uses pictures or symbols) will use a *code key*, or translation, to help them understand these early forms of communication.

Some of the most elegant codes are the simplest. See if you can decipher this popular phrase:

IBQQZ CJSUIEBZ UP ZPV ...

Doesn't make much sense, does it? But it would if you knew the key. Try moving each letter one step backward in the alphabet and you'll have something that only happens once a year! (Still stumped? Look for the answer on page 124.)

Let's Cook!

Write a letter to a friend using code. You can include the key or even send it ahead of time. Both of you can use the same key (make one up together!) to write back and forth, and only you and your friend will understand the message (unless the key falls into enemy hands, that is!).

(Still stumped? Look for the answer on page 124.)

E-E-E ELL-GLSS! *

Kiwyrhlimx.*

*go back 4 letters

CHEF'S TIPS *Remember that for a code to work, both parties must have the same key!*

Recipe

serves: 1 player (and a pen-pal friend!)

ingredients:
- Pencil and paper (or email)
- Envelope and stamp

skill level LOW MEDIUM HIGH

Brain Candy

You use codes in more ways than you may be aware of. How about when you receive a letter in the mail (zip code), or a grocery clerk scans a package of gum (bar code)? Can you think of other codes you use on a daily basis?

code talkers, cryptograph, encryption, hieroglyph, Morse code, zip code

Code Talkers

During World War II, Philip Johnston (who was raised on a Navajo reservation) suggested that the military use the Navajo language as a code because of its complexity and limited usage. By the time the war in the Pacific ended, more than 400 Navajo "code talkers" had conveyed important military messages back and forth.

After the war, the Japanese government admitted to breaking most of the codes used by the United States, but it never cracked the Navajo code.

Baxter Says:

Codes are fun for kids to play with, but they should never be used to keep secrets that harm or make fun of other people.

Smervitz & Gatoosh (serve up your own words!)

For jeeble pock and roody mets
A fortish blitz would bander
That in akreen the mootish haddy fly.

Does the sentence above make any sense to you? No? Well, it shouldn't. I just made it up (imagine getting *paid* to write like this!).

There are some recognizable words, like **for** and **would**, but many are totally unrecognizable. I chose them because I thought they sounded funny, and because they had a certain rhythm (known by poets as *meter*).

I've always felt that the best way to understand words is to play with them a little, and by doing so I managed to (in this activity, anyway) do away with most rules for spelling.

(Actually, I wish you were standing over my shoulder right now, watching me type. The spell check in my word processor is going absolutely nuts! I wonder how you turn this thing off ...)

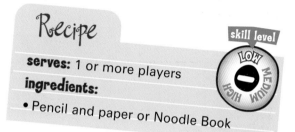

Recipe

skill level

serves: 1 or more players

ingredients:
• Pencil and paper or Noodle Book

Would pupsy like some badle cravitz?

Let's Cook!

Write your own lyrics to a song, or a poem to yourself, using made-up words. Be sure to use some real words to "tie" your piece together, so it's not completely unrecognizable. Then let friends or relatives try to read what you've written out loud. Watch for the surprised looks on their faces!

If your readers ask you what this is all about, ask them what they think the words mean. Explain that you're making up your own words and trying to be creative (just like the author of this book!).

Brain Candy

Can making up your own words make you famous?
Check out the poem on the next page. If you've ever heard of Lewis Carroll or the Jabberwock or Alice in Wonderland, then I guess the answer is yes!

Jabberwock Soup Stock

W e throw lots of odd things into soups, hoping that — if we cook them long enough — something tasty will result. Lewis Carroll (best known for his books *Alice's Adventures in Wonderland* and *Through the Looking-Glass*) was a master at mixing things up. In *Through the Looking-Glass*, he penned a poem that has become a standard for made-up or nonsense words.

Jabberwocky

By Lewis Carroll (1832–98), from *Through the Looking-Glass, and What Alice Found There* (London: Macmillan and Co., 1872)

'TWAS brillig, and the slithy toves
Did gyre and gimble in the wabe;
All mimsy were the borogoves,
And the mome raths outgrabe.

"Beware the Jabberwock, my son!
The jaws that bite, the claws that catch!
Beware the Jubjub bird, and shun
The frumious Bandersnatch!"

He took his vorpal sword in hand:
Long time the manxome foe he sought —
So rested he by the Tumtum tree,
And stood awhile in thought.

And, as in uffish thought he stood,
The Jabberwock, with eyes of flame,
Came whiffling through the tulgey wood,
And burbled as it came!

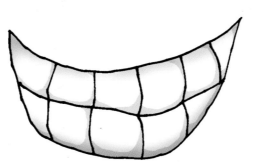

One, two! One, two! And through and through
The vorpal blade went snicker-snack!
He left it dead, and with its head
He went galumphing back.

"And, hast thou slain the Jabberwock?
Come to my arms, my beamish boy!
O frabjous day! Callooh! Callay!"
He chortled in his joy.

'Twas brillig, and the slithy toves
Did gyre and gimble in the wabe;
All mimsy were the borogoves,
And the mome raths outgrabe.

occupy: to possess a flaky pastry dish.

Cook Up Your Own Language

What could be more difficult than trying to learn all of the (often senseless) rules that go along with the English language? I guess it would be making up a language of your own!

Sound crazy? Well, what else have you got to do? There sure isn't anything on TV (I've checked!).

People actually have created their own languages, sometimes based on a language they were already familiar with, and sometimes just from pure imagination (see TOLKIEN TALK and KLINGON CHATTER, page 49).

snatgimple
murple
bervish
terly

PUNZLES®

An Easy Beginning

To start, choose some everyday words that you use a lot and make up new words for them, and — as we did in SMERVITZ & GATOOSH (page 46) — use common words (such as **for** and **to** and **with**) to "glue" them together to form sentences.

Once you've written down or memorized most of your new words, create new "glue words." The only problem you'll have with your made-up language is that you will need to teach it to other kids before they can understand you.

Sound like a lot of work? *That* is totally up to you. Before you decide, meet some people who thought it would be a lot of fun. Read on ...

KEYWORD KABOBS

dialect, grammar, idioms, jargon, linguistics, vernacular

noro lim,
noro lim,
Asfaloth!

Tolkien Talk

Unless you've been living under a rock for the last few years, you are probably aware of J.R.R. Tolkien's wonderful books *The Hobbit* and "The Lord of the Rings" trilogy. Tolkien was fascinated with *runes,* or symbols used in Old English, so it was perfectly natural for him to come up with languages (Elvish, Orcish, and Dwarvish, to name a few) unique to his books. (The space here is much too short to go into a lot of detail about his languages, but for a complete guide to those, see Appendix E of the final "The Lord of the Rings" book, *The Return of the King.*) There are many people (and even college classes) today who study Tolkien's made-up languages!

lunatic: a small parasitic insect that only comes out during a full moon.

Klingon Chatter

Countless *Star Trek* movies have been made (and probably are *still* being made) that would not be quite as interesting without the help of Marc Okrand, the writer who invented the Klingon language heard first in *Star Trek III: "The Search for Spock."*

Klingon has been used in *Star Trek* movies ever since. There's even a book called *The Klingon Dictionary* that describes the grammar and vocabulary of the language.

Okrand, like Tolkien, is not just another word hack (like myself). He has a Ph.D. in linguistics and specializes in American Indian languages of the West Coast.

qaStaH nug?

Not much. You?

Spaced-Out Spread

So med a yI'll wi shup on as tar an dwake up whe ret he cloud saref arbe hind me. Whe retro uble smelt likel em on drop saw ay abo vet he chim neyt opst hat's whe reyo u'll fin dme.

Have you ever heard the term "space cadet"? It usually refers to someone who's deep in thought or has a faraway look in his eyes. And before you can ask, yes, I have been called a space cadet.

But space is used in other ways as well. Not only do we travel in space now, but without it our language could become very messy. I will demonstrate.

Fourscoreandsevenyearsagoourfathersbroughtforthonthiscontinentanewnationcon ceivedinlibertyanddedicatedtothepropositionthatallmenarecreatedequal.

You might (or might not) recognize this text as the beginning of Abraham Lincoln's famous Gettysburg Address, delivered at Gettysburg, Pennsylvania, on November 19, 1863, during the Civil War. If you do as I have done and take out all the spaces, the text becomes almost unrecognizable. And if you added spaces in unusual places, it might read like this:

F ours core ands even yea rsa goo urfa the rsb rought for thont hiscon tin entan ewnati oncon ceive din lib ertyand ded I cat edtot he prop osi tiont hat allme narec rea ted equal.

Did you notice that there are actually new words popping up with the different spacing? You could change the way I've spaced it and find even more words hidden in the text. So, cook up your own spread!

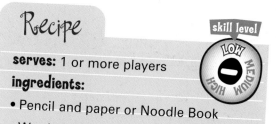

Recipe

skill level

serves: 1 or more players

ingredients:

• Pencil and paper or Noodle Book

• Words to a famous song or poem

Let's Cook!

Take a familiar song or poem, and write it down once without any spaces. Next, write it again using spaces wherever you think they should go. To make it as confusing as possible for someone else to read, try to break the letters where they will form new, real words.

Hand your new creation to a friend to see if she can decipher what the original verse was.

Try this along with CREPES OF WRATH, page 54.

There are misspelled words all around you (I'm hoping that you've noticed!), and like mush, they are not very pretty. As an example, the owners of many convenience stores have found countless ways to spell the word **quick**. As in **kwik, quik, kwick, quic,** and so on. They do this to separate themselves from their competitors.

There are occasions, however, when incorrect spelling is used for a perfectly good effect. Take a look at the funny pages of your newspaper sometime and see if you can find comics that use misspelled words on purpose.

Let's Cook!

Take the Misspelling Challenge. For one entire day, challenge your whole family to a misspelling competition. No, you don't misspell words yourself, but you *find* misspellings. To add to the fun, use a camera to take pictures of all the misspelled signs you see. And don't forget to look in the newspaper. See any headlines that are misspelled? Uh-oh! Be sure to check the advertisements, too! Who's the top misspeller spotter in your household?

Recipe

skill level
LOW
MEDIUM
HIGH

serves: 1 or more players (get the whole family involved!)

ingredients:
- Road signs, restaurant and fast-food signs, TV, newspapers — wherever you see words!
- Pencil and paper or Noodle Book

Famous Misspeller Mush

One popular comic strip that uses misspelled words for effect is Wiley Miller's *Non-Sequitur*. In this strip from November 2003, Miller uses phonetics to emphasize the manner in which Danae's grandmother speaks.

Back in the early 1900s, George Herriman wrote and drew a cartoon strip called *Krazy Kat,* which featured a cat (Krazy), a mouse (Ignatz), and a dog (Offissa Pupp), among other colorful characters. Throughout the long history of the strip, the cat was notorious for his pronunciation of words, which even today take more than a little thought to decipher.

Spell the Beans!

Misspell words? On purpose?! Omigosh! What will your teachers say? After all the hours they've spent correcting your spelling; after your teachers have tested and retested you on the proper way to spell just about every word in the dictionary?

Sure! Why not?

Let's Cook!

Write a letter to a friend about your vacation or about everyday things. And when you do, *misspell every word possible!* But here's the catch: Write using *phonetics*, or a representation of how words sound in speech. The person you're writing to can sound out the message, often with hilarious results!

You can also do the same with an email message (I sent and received lots of these as I wrote this book!). Just be sure not to use the spell-check tool before you send your message.

> Deer Soozie,
> Howl ar yoo? Eye have bin phine. Wee tuke a vakaishun thiss yeer and wint two Niagara Phalls n Noo Yorke. Mie bruthr gawt sik n hour cahr and mawm sed hee aight to much Pawpkorn. Right sune.
> Yore Frend,
> —Brawnie

KEYWORD KABOBS

dipthong, phonetics, phonology, plosive speech

relief: what trees do in the spring.

The word **dictionary**
with pronunciation symbols,

primary
(or strongest)
stress

did
shy
kin
red
nine
real
tip
suppose
easy

ˈdik-shə-ˌner-ē

syllable
division

secondary
(or next-strongest)
stress

and spelled phonetically.

dik-shuh-nair-ee

Phonetics is a system of sounds that we use to process patterns of speech, which is especially helpful when you consider how complex some languages are (like English — see PANFRIED PROBLEMS, page 23).

If you're having trouble coming up with the phonetic sound of a word, there's always the dictionary, where you will find the phonetic spelling for every word. Check it out!

PUNZLES©

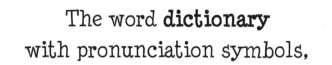

So then Little Red Riding Hood says to the wolf, "My, what big EYES you have grandma!" "All the better to see you with" says the wolf. Then suddenly she spots the huge teeth and says, "My, what big choppers you have, Granny!" Well, you can just guess what happens next...

Baxter Says:

Me? Yow!

Kids as well as adults should always try to spell words correctly — unless you are playing a word game, of course. A properly spelled word is the best form of communication. And before you can have fun misspelling words, you'll need to know the correct spelling. Am I write?

Crepes of Wrath (words baked in words)

A *crepe* (pronounced KRAPE, rhymes with **grape**) is a very thin pancake usually stuffed with other food and rolled up. Did you know you can find many words that are often rolled in other words?

As in SPACED-OUT SPREAD (page 50), there are many instances when longer words are made of shorter words:

INspiRATiON

I've capitalized three words (**in**, **rat**, and **on**) that are wrapped up in the word **inspiration** already. Can you find any others? The trick here is that —

unlike anagrams, page 30 — the letters of the hidden words must *follow one another*, and not be mixed up out of order. (There are at least seven hidden words that I found.)

Let's practice a little with these words (the number of hidden words I found is in the parentheses after each word):

neurotransmitter (9)
mathematics (12)
beforehand (12)
copyrightable (9)
unintelligible (4)
reallocation (6)
extraterrestrial (11)

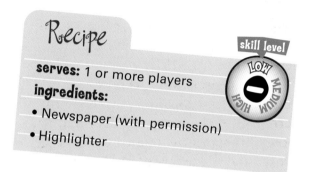

Let's Cook!

Take a page from the newspaper, and using a highlighter, see how many word crepes you can find. Be sure to check the advertisements, too!

The only rule, remember, is that all the letters of the words must be consecutive (following one another in order).

Taste Test

Can you find as many words-hidden-in-words as I have in the examples? Check your answers with mine on page 124.

republican;
rep, pub, public,
can, an, a...

N*

*Why **N** instead of **Z**? Baxter is only half asleep...

Kangaroo Word Waffles

Recipe

skill level HIGH MEDIUM LOW

serves: 1 or more players
ingredients:
• Words, anywhere you see them!

Kangaroo words are a lot like CREPES OF WRATH, page 54, but take the recipe to a whole new level.

In a kangaroo word, the word that's hidden (often called the *joey*, after the term for a baby kangaroo in its mother's pouch) is somehow related to the larger word, and the letters of the hidden word should be separated by at least one other letter *and* should appear in the correct order.

I'll give some examples by highlighting the joey in capital letters:

recLInE
SAlVagE
encoURaGE
StOCKingS

Kangaroo words are not very easy to come up with. It is possible to find some examples if you search the Internet (with an adult's permission, see page 108), but most simply come from careful observation.

If you can find any kangaroo words, slap yourself five and be sure to write them down somewhere. You could become the world's first expert at cooking KANGAROO WORD WAFFLES!

I want to play with other joeys 'cause I'm lONeLY!

renown: what you have to do if your teacher says that you've used the wrong noun.

Get Out of the Kitchen

O kay, it's time for a break. It's getting hot in the kitchen, the sink is full of dirty dishes, and we've flat-out made Emeril jealous. So let's put away the pencils and the Noodle Book for a moment, and take a look at PUNZLES® on a whole new level.

PUNZLES® (so far) have been single images that you've been asked to figure out. Well, in this version, I give you the words or phrases, but you have to find the images that represent those words. I know what you're thinking: "Michael Kline is a few french fries short of a Happy Meal." Alas, I will explain.

Highlighted in **RED** in the following story are words that describe items in the image (next page), but instead of being literal clues, they are phonetic puns. As an example, for the words *serial killer*, think "*cereal killer*." See how many words and images you can match. The answers are on page 124.

> The American was no amateur. He took his catsup and notebook, readied his escape, then began a quality search for the serial killer. A gigantic job lay before him, and without the correct apparel, things could quickly mushroom. His forehead ached, and he knew that the keyboard in his office was no help now. A philosopher might have interpreted the message on the company letterhead differently, but for now it was business as usual.

Film Flambé (movie title acronym madness)

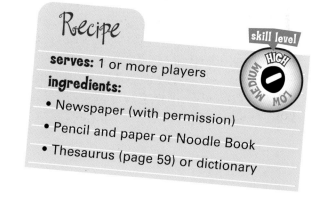

flambé (FLAUM-bay): a cooking term that involves drenching food with an edible ignitable liquid such as rum or brandy, then setting it on fire.

acronym (ACK-roe-nim): a word formed from the initial letters of a name.

Any idea where I'm headed with this? Well FYI (for your information), I want you to grab your GA (guardian angel), put on a CD (compact disk), and play this game ASAP (as soon as possible)!

Acronyms are everywhere! If you start to listen, you'll hear just how many acronyms are in use today.

So, my fine young lexical buddies, let's play a game I like to call FILM FLAMBÉ!

Let's Cook!

Find the movie section of the newspaper, and pick out a movie that's currently playing (or perhaps you can think of the title of a well-known movie).

Take the letters of the title and write them down the left side of the page. Now think of words that begin with those letters. See if you can come up with a phrase that describes the movie.

I'll do one first to show you how it's done.

T = TIMON
H = HELPS
E = ELFIN
L = LION
I = INHERIT
O = OPPRESSED
N = NATURE
K = KINGDOM.
I = IS
N = NOW
G = GLAD.

Hey, no one says it has to be pretty! The important thing is to have fun.

Synonym Rolls (or why Mother Goose is upset with me)

Have you ever made synonym rolls? They're really quite easy to prepare. You just take something that everyone recognizes (in this case, a nursery rhyme) and cover it with something else. I'll give an example. Can you recognize it? (Answer on page 124.)

Yo, diddle, diddle,
The feline and the violin;
The bovine leapt over the lunar body.
The wee canine chortled
To witness such athleticism,
And the platter left home at a quick
   pace with the scoop-style silverware.

Let's Cook!

Take a familiar story or phrase and rewrite it using synonyms. When your SYNONYM ROLLS are done, put them on a clean piece of paper with a clue to their origin (movie title, nursery rhyme, or song). Hand them to a friend to see if he can uncover the true meaning.

pseudonym, synonym,
synonymous, thesaurus

DaD! CaN We Go see A Succession of Calamitous Circumstances TONIGHT afTER DINNER?

Recipe

serves: 1 or more players

ingredients:

- Favorite poem, short story, nursery rhyme, book or movie title
- Pencil and paper or Noodle Book
- Thesaurus or dictionary (optional)

skill level

LOW MEDIUM HIGH

Taste Test

Can you recognize the real name of this epic three-part movie?

The Potentate of the Metallic Circular Enclosures

(Answer on page 124.)

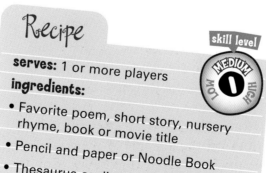

Baxter Says:

Me? Yow!

A synonym is a word that has nearly the same meaning as another word, and a thesaurus *is a book of synonyms. A thesaurus is a large book with many interesting words, such as* **tuna**.

For more on reference books, see page 123.

wonderful would become **twoderful**, **forehead** would become **fivehead**, and so on.

Let's inflate the first paragraph of Abraham Lincoln's Gettysburg Address (page 50) and see what happens.

Fivescore and eight years ago our fathers brought fifth on this conelevenent a new nation, conceived in liberty and dedicnined to the proposition that all men are crenined equal.

Now, you try one (I mean, *two!*).

Let's Cook!

Find a short story, poem, song, or nursery rhyme and inflate it. If you can't find one, make one up. It will sound just as silly.

High-Carb Word Pop-Ups

There are all kinds of diets these days, most of which are preaching to people to cut back on things. But we're going to do things a little differently (go figure!). We're going to *add* some things!

Danish composer and humorist Victor Borge (1909–2000) would often tell a story to his audience using what he called *inflationary language*. Wherever he found a number (or a word or syllable that almost sounded like a number) in the story, he would increase the number by one. As an example,

quarter horse: a mechanical steed in front of a grocery store that you can ride for 25¢.

Low-F@ Symbol S&wich

L et's put together a simple lunch that uses symbols instead of letters. Wh@ am I talking about? Allow me to explain.

There are many symbols that we use in place of words in order to simplify our communication. The symbol @, meaning "at," has become very popular with the coming of the Internet and email. But *I* see it (and other symbols) as a fun way to use the letters A and T together.

Some other symbol words include **1/2** ("half"), **1/4** ("quarter"), **&** ("and"), **#** ("pound," also "number"), **–** ("minus"), **+** ("plus"), **X** ("times"), **.** ("period"), **<** ("is less than"), **>** ("is greater than"), **•** ("bullet"), **¢** ("cents," or phonetically "sense"), **—** ("dash"), and so on. You can even use *numbers* as words.

ideogram, logogram, typographic accents

Using these definitions, can you read the following story?

Mikey woke up 1 morning with a #ing headache. "This > the 1 I had just yesterday," he thought, but put on his clothes, slipped in2 his s&als, & shot 4 the door like a •. "There are X when a kid needs 2 be outside," he said. When he arrived @ his s&box, he noticed something shiny. "It's a brand-new 1/4!" he shouted. "But how did it get out here? This doesn't make any ¢."

"Mikey!" shouted his mom, "Come in & feed the c@!"

"Do I 1/2 2?" he answered.

"Yes, & right now."

"R@s," he muttered, and —ed off 4 the house.

Let's Cook!

Write a short story using as many symbol words as possible. Don't forget to use number words, too, just 2 make it fun 4 every1 who reads it.

CHEF'S TIPS *It might be easier to make a LOW-F@ SYMBOL S&WICH if you write down your story first, then go back over it to find places where symbols can replace letters and words.*

Recipe
skill level
LOW MEDIUM HIGH

serves: 1 or more players
ingredients:
• Pencil and paper or Noodle Book

@-choo!

Uh oh! Sounds like a virus.

License Pl8 Pie

Here's something that's easy to cook up, and anytime you're in the car with nothing to do, you'll likely taste many examples of LICENSE PL8 PIE (also called Pl8 Speak).

There are many words and numbers that, when used phonetically (that is, the way they *sound*), can produce a language all their own.

With the introduction of vanity license plates (personalized plates for the car), it became important to get messages out in as few letters as possible, because many states allow only seven letters. So people began to be creative (or CRE8IVE).

I'll give you some popular Pl8 phrases and their solutions to start you out. Figure it out; then check your answers on page 124.

ICU812

IRIGHTI

10SNE1

AV8R

CUL8ER

Let's Cook!

Write a story of your own using Pl8 Speak, then hand it to another person and ask him to read it (when he has time; it may not be easy!). You can use symbols such as periods and commas for punctuation, but not for sounds. You may want to give your readers the solution on a separate piece of paper, just in case!

rebus, vanity plates, William Steig

Check out William Steig's wonderful books *CDB!* and *CDC?* Not only R they fun 2 read, but they R A 1derful way 2 learn Pl8 Speak.

Note: This one is better read in a rear-view mirror...

Mirror Word Macaroni & Cheese
(& how it reflects on you)

Here's a very simple recipe for word fun that almost anyone can whip up. And just like the real macaroni and cheese, all it takes is a little *stirring*.

As a wee tyke, I took great pleasure in sending friends letters that were, well, not your usual, everyday letters. And though a lot of creativity on the envelope (as I found out) could cause the post office some grief, I felt that the contents were fair game.

I also thought that your typical "This is what I did this summer" letter was b-o-o-o-o-ring, so whenever I conversed with someone through the mail, I tried to make it interesting. And here is one way that you can, too!

Recipe

skill level

serves: 1 or more players

ingredients:
- Pencil and paper
- Window
- Envelope and stamp

Let's Cook!

Write a short letter to someone, then flip it (left to right, not top to bottom) and tape it to a window. You should be able to see through it, but all the writing will be backward. Now, take another piece of paper, hold it over the first letter, and copy the words so that your new letter reads in *reverse*.

When your friend receives the letter in the mail, she'll need to hold it up to a mirror to read it. Or, she can hold the letter backward up to a light to see your "secret message."

Brain Candy

Have you ever noticed that a photo of you might look a little odd, like something is just a bit out of place? Don't be frightened if you have. Most of us see ourselves every day in a mirror, but that is not the real us. It is a mirror (or flopped) image. Take a photo of yourself sometime and look at it while you're looking in the mirror. What you see may surprise you! Is your hair parted on a different side? Have most of your freckles traded places? Well, say hello to the person everyone else sees — everyone else, that is, but you!

Finely Chop One Newspaper Page ...

Recipe

skill level

serves: 1 or more players

ingredients:
- Newspaper comics (with permission)
- Scissors
- Clear tape

Many of us like to read the comics in the newspaper. I used to think, "What if one of the characters in a certain strip was using the words from another strip?"

The more I thought about it, the funnier it got. So let's check out your dicing skills and ...

Let's Cook!

Read through the comics section (use some from days past if necessary) and make note of places where you think one cartoon character's words will work in another strip. Cut out the words and place them carefully over the words of another strip.

Mix and match before you tape anything down, and if it helps, cut out pictures and mix them up, too. You may want to tape the whole thing to a new piece of paper. Show the result to an adult, and he may even offer to frame it for you! I guarantee that it will be an original.

And for only $14.95 you too can love each other like A SAUCE MADE ENTIRELY FROM 40 yards and 3 interceptions in Pakistan where citizens met with the best kitchen appliance ever!

flypaper: a boarding pass to an airline.

Baxter Says:

Me? Yow!

Always ask permission for games that are played with "grown-up" toys. (Yes, the remote is a toy in my opinion.) Even a remote control won't last forever, and the batteries give out in no time!

Remote-Control Coleslaw

Coleslaw is a salad made of finely shredded cabbage (which, like this activity, can be stinky if not properly prepared). So how would you like to shred something like a few hundred words with a TV remote control?

Because I am a guy (and all guys know this), I take great pride in seeing just how fast I can flip through the channels, taking less than a second to recognize a good show from a bad one. In doing so, I began to see (or rather *hear*) something fun going on.

I then began "surfing" with my eyes closed, just listening for the words or phrases that *when strung together* were often funnier than anything on television.

It's pretty easy to "shred" some dialogue, but please, *always* do it with permission!

Recipe

skill level
LOW MEDIUM HIGH

serves: 1 player (preferably in an empty room, because this game can be very annoying if you aren't playing!)

ingredients:
• 1 TV with remote control

Let's Cook!

Turn the TV volume to a moderate level, and start to "surf," paying attention to the phrases that are produced using "shredded" sentences.

After a bit, you will learn to change channels between the natural pauses that the actors take, and you will start to hear some pretty funny stuff.

CHEF'S TIPS *If you want to share your recipe with friends, make a recording of your REMOTE-CONTROL COLESLAW and play it back.*

Portrait Pickles (jar your friends)

Joseph, who's designing this book

Vickie, my wonderful wife

Jennifer, my friend in New York

Recipe

skill level

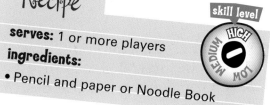

serves: 1 or more players
ingredients:
• Pencil and paper or Noodle Book

Let's Cook!

Using the name of a friend (it helps if the name has more than three letters, and sometimes using her last name helps, too), rearrange the letters by rotating them, turning them upside down or backward, making them bigger or smaller, and making some in capitals and others in lowercase letters (because their shapes are often different). Pretty soon you will have a portrait of that person's name.

It may take a while to master this recipe, but once you begin to see how different letters can make different shapes, your PORTRAIT PICKLES will cook up in a jiffy.

CHEF'S TIPS *If you have access to a computer drawing program, you can rearrange the letters even faster and make a nice printout, too. You may also be able to choose different typefaces (type styles).*

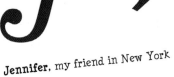

Taste Test ???

From where you sit right now, can you spot a logo for a company that uses one or more of its initials? (Hint: Look on the cover of this book. Answer on page 124.)

Earlier (page 14, to be exact), I discussed how important the letters of the alphabet are when it comes to playing word games. But did you know a person's name can not only be spelled with letters, but *drawn* with them as well?

Wait! Don't call a doctor for me just yet. Let me explain.

The logos of many companies are made from the company's initials. So why not do the same with your name? Draw a picture with the letters!

Undergrounder Upside-Down Cake

"If you can't raise the bridge, then lower the river." I'm not sure who said that, but it means that there is always more than one way to look at things, and among those things, I include words and phrases.

Undergrounders are words or phrases that work on two levels. Most of the words used as UNFORTUNATE COOKIES are undergrounders. They are the result of taking a word and turning it upside down (several times) until a newer, more interesting definition is found.

Here are a few undergrounders and their definitions to start you off:

gargoyle: an olive-flavored mouthwash (because it sounds like *gargle* and olive *oil*).

occupy: the job of a pastry chef (because it sounds like *occupation* and *pie*).

See how it works? Try cooking up some of your own.

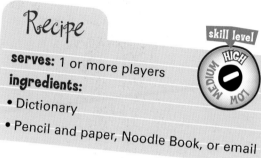

Recipe

serves: 1 or more players

ingredients:
- Dictionary
- Pencil and paper, Noodle Book, or email

skill level

Let's Cook!

Look for words in the dictionary that might have a different meaning if they were combinations of two or more words.

Write down the correct spelling of the word, then write down its new definition. Bravo!

CHEF'S TIPS *If you have trouble finding undergrounder words, look for longer words and just keep repeating them to yourself over and over (forget what the real meaning is for a moment). The key ingredient here is imagination! Oh,* **imagination:** *a country where everyone is required to be creative (***imagine + nation***). See how easy this becomes?*

Greenwich:
The person who captured Dorothy and Toto.

Baxter Says:
Me? Yow!

Playing with words and coming up with new definitions is lots of fun. While you're at it, surprise your teachers or parents by memorizing the real meaning of those words. You'll be a vocabulary pro!

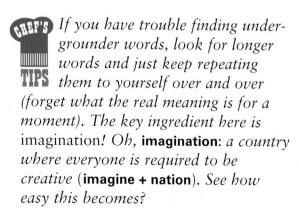

Tabloid Turkey Tapioca (a.k.a. headline herrings)

Despite their best intentions, newspaper copy editors often let some funny headline accidents slip through. If you published something as large and complex as a newspaper every day, you might make a few mistakes, too. Some of these grammar goofs are quite hilarious!

Two Soviet Ships Collide — One Dies
Squad Helps Dog Bite Victim
Teacher Strikes Idle Kids
Man Charged With Battery

Can you figure out what each headline was intending? Obviously, a man was not charged with a battery, but he was charged (as in court) with battery (which is a civil offense).

Let's Cook!

Look through your newspaper for those occasional HEADLINE HERRINGS, and make a note of them. Or, better yet, cut them out and glue or tape them into a notebook or scrapbook. Put the date below the entry and jot down the name of the paper you found it in. When you've found several, share them with friends or compare them.

You might even want to drop a note to the editor of the paper (look on the Editorial or Opinion page), letting the editor know what you've found, and perhaps suggesting a solution for future such headlines.

CHEF'S TIPS *If you collect a lot of these, make copies and bind them up to give as holiday or birthday gifts. People love them!*

Zeugma Zest

Harold knew all along that someday he would find the true meaning of life and his shoes.

Taste Test

There is a zeugma in the paragraph that begins with "Get the hang ..." Can you find it? (Answer on page 124.)

Recipe

skill level: HIGH / MEDIUM / LOW

serves: 1 or more players

ingredients:

• Pencil and paper or Noodle Book

What's a *zeugma* (ZOOG-ma)? It's a phrase or sentence in which a word is applied to two or more phrases in different, often humorous, ways.

Confused? Join the club. Perhaps an example will help:

Steve decided to write on Clinton and a piece of paper.

KEYWORD KABOBS

syllepsis, zeugma

Say what? Well, see how I used the words **write on** and applied them to both **Clinton** and a **piece of paper**? Let's try another ...

The coach was losing the game and her temper.

Get the hang of it? Great! You're ready to add some zest to your everyday language with a few zeugmas of your own. With a little practice, maybe you'll get smarter and invited to more parties!

Let's Cook!

There is no logical way to come up with a good zeugma short of just listening for patterns of speech that could *use* a good zeugma. Remember, a great deal of wordplay comes about as a result of good listening skills!

Brain Candy

Zeugos **is the** Greek word for "yoked."

A Pair of Paradox Pears

Did you ever wonder why we **park** on **drive**ways and **drive** on **park**ways? Why do I say my alarm clock has gone **off** when it has actually turned **on**? Why do we have **noses** that **run** and **feet** that **smell**? And what about these two words: **Civil War**?

These are some examples of *word paradoxes*. A paradox (not two surgeons!) is a contradictory statement (and is yet another reason why the English language is so difficult for foreign people to learn).

To properly prepare pairs of paradox pears (how's that for a tongue twister?), keep your ears open!

KEYWORD KABOBS

antinomy, Goldwynisms, oxymoron, Seinfeldisms, word paradox

groan: what an adult should be.

Let's Cook!

Listen for examples of word paradoxes and write them down. Share them with friends via email, and maybe they'll return the favor by sending some to you. While you're hunting these down, can you see why English may not be the easiest language for foreign people to learn?

There is no EGG in eggplant.

There is no HAM in hamburger.

WHY IS A BOXING "RING" SQUARE?

Brain Candy

Here are a few more examples of paradoxes for some more fun:

When a house burns **up**, it burns **down**?

You fill **out** a form by filling it **in**?

Why is something transported by car called a **ship**ment, and something transported by boat called **car**go?

The weather can be **hot as heck** one day and **cold as heck** the next?

If lawyers want to be taken seriously, why is their business called a **practice**?

PUNZLES®

Dude!

Dude!

rampage: a place in a book where you read about male sheep.

Jigsaw Jam

Sticky, but delicious! That's how I would describe this recipe. And once you've served it to a friend, you'll likely have it served back to you.

Over the course of many years, I have made JIGSAW JAM for countless friends, and you might be surprised to learn that — unlike the jelly that's in your fridge — my jams have been in the drawers and cupboards of friends and family for many years (yuck, huh?). Before you start seeing this whole thing as a science experiment gone bad, perhaps we should take a closer look at the recipe.

Let's Cook!

Find a used jigsaw puzzle (I look for puzzles at the local thrift store — they're very inexpensive), and assemble it on top of one of the pieces of cardboard.

Recipe

skill level!

LOW MEDIUM HIGH

serves: 1 or more players

ingredients:

- New or used jigsaw puzzle, preferably less than 100 pieces
- 2 large pieces of stiff cardboard
- Adult helper
- Pencils or fine-tipped marker

With the help of an adult, place the other piece of cardboard on top of the completed puzzle, and very carefully turn it over, keeping the puzzle in one piece.

On the back side of the puzzle, write a letter to a friend telling her why you value her friendship, or something about why you're thinking of her (I like to write my letters in a circle, as shown, just to throw my readers off the trail a little).

Disassemble the puzzle, put it back in the box, and maybe even gift wrap it. Then give it to your friend without telling her what it is. (You may not hear back from her for some time!)

If you want to be a real stinker (like me), carefully peel the picture from the cover of the box, giving your friend an extra challenge!

Brain Candy

Jigsaw puzzles can be traced back to the 1700s, when the mapmakers of Europe pasted their maps onto pieces of wood, then cut them apart (most likely to make them easier to store aboard ships) — a far cry from Flash-based jigsaw puzzles found on the Internet today.

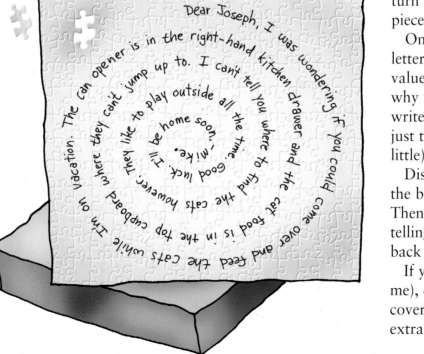

Chapter Fore

DEEP-FRIED DICTION FOR TWO
(OR MORE!)

TABLE NO.	DINERS	SERVING NO.	004

The knock, knockwurst is on the grill,
The lemonade is cold,
So call your friends to have some fun
With oxymorons bold!

"Your Pan's on Fire, your puns are dire!"
You'll tell your verbose buds,
So twist your tongues, warm up your lungs,
And launch some dooner spuds!

Soda Pop Swap

Once you've discovered the fun of *homonyms* — those words that sound alike but are spelled differently and mean different things, like **bare** and **bear**; **sew** and **so**; **I**, **eye**, and **aye** (see HOMONYM GRITS, page 42) — you're well on your way to becoming a culinary word wizard, first-class. If homonyms make you happy, you might like to whip up a recipe I call SODA POP SWAP. It's a great way to explore and learn many different homonyms.

Let's Cook!

Choose one player to cover his ears (or pop in the earbuds and listen to some rap music on a portable player) while you and a partner compose a sentence using at least two homonyms, using the phrase **soda pop** in place of the homonyms. For example: *Right after I* ***soda pop*** *supper, I went to the library and read until* ***soda pop*** *o'clock.*

See how I used **soda pop** in place of the homonyms **ate** and **eight**?

_____

homophone

I can tie a clove hitch soda pop, but soda pop right now.

Have the third player listen up and pay attention to the sentence. If he correctly identifies the proper words, it becomes someone else's turn to be the Guesser. Award one point for each correct guess, and play to five points — or just play for the pure fun of it.

 CHEF'S TIPS *SODA POP SWAP is a great game to play in the car to make time fly when you are stuck in traffic.*

Recipe

skill level

serves: 3 or more players

ingredients:

• Just your imagination!

Brain Candy

Homonyms are worth their weight in gold when creating great puns (page 76) and knock-knock jokes (next page)!

Baxter Says:
Me? Yow!

If your nose knows no way
To make sense of scents,
Then what the maid made
Could taste as wood would.
Can you find all the homonyms?
(Answers on page 124.)

Knock, Knockwurst (hot dog!)

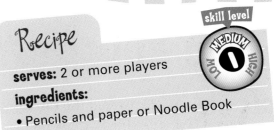

Recipe

skill level: MEDIUM

serves: 2 or more players

ingredients:
- Pencils and paper or Noodle Book

Boy, where would the United States be today without millions of kids running around telling knock-knock jokes? Most pint-sized punsters I've met have begun their careers by telling KKs (as I fondly refer to them).

This type of wordplay involves *punning*, or making a play on words in which you use two or more different ideas in a single expression, in a way (and this is the important part!) that seems humorous to the person making up the pun. Sometimes it is even funny to other people (but not always!). You probably know some knock-knock jokes already.

Here are some classics to get you thinking:

Knock, knock!
Who's there?
Lettuce.
Lettuce who?
Lettuce in, we're freezing!

Knock, knock.
Who's there?
Water.
Water who?
Water you doing in my house?

There is no easy way to teach a person how to create a knock-knock joke. Just listen for words (or combinations of words) that sound like other words. As with cooking hot dogs, once you know how, they are really easy to prepare!

Let's Cook!

Gather a pal or two on the front porch or under the shade of a tree, and just start cooking. If you know some KK jokes already, tell them to get all of you in the right mindset.

Take turns playing your jokes on each other. Then take a vote and decide who made up the best knock-knock joke. Here's a clue: The worst jokes are usually the best! Declare that person the wiener. (Oops, I meant *winner*!) Write down your best jokes so you can remember to use them again.

double entendre,
knock knock, puns, punning

Pun-ishing Prune Pastry

Puns! Some of the most fun word games involve puns and punning. And here's a little tip worth repeating for you mighty word warriors: The best puns are the worst. That is, if someone groans after you say your pun, then you've got a winner!

You will also find that most puns are found to be the funniest by the people who are telling them. Puns are also considered by many to be the lowliest form of humor. (Yay!)

If you get to be a world-class punster, consider yourself in good company, along with the likes of James Joyce, Ogden Nash, and (especially) William Shakespeare.

Let me give you a little lesson on how to prepare your own bad jokes.

~KEYWORD~
~KABOBS~

---

idiom, James Joyce, Ogden Nash, pun, punster, William Shakespeare, witticism

behind: the stinger.

WHAT DO YOU USE TO FIGURE THE AREA OF A FRUIT?

APPLE PI?

What do you call an honest hotdog?

Frank?

WHAT'S THE MAIN INGREDIENT IN A CAKE FOR ELEPHANTS?

PEANUT BATTER?

NAME A MOVIE THAT STARS AN ICE-SKATING HOBBIT.

LORD OF THE RINKS?

Do you have a duck pay with a check or a credit card?

Neither. You put it on his bill.

What do you call an $85 Big Mac?

A JEEZ burger.

Brain Candy

An **idiom** is phrase or expression that is unique to a given language, as in the phrase "Go figure," which I use to mean "that was pretty obvious." If you begin to listen for idioms, you'll hear them used quite often, too.

Recipe

skill level

serves: 2 or more players

ingredients:

- Pencils and paper or Noodle Book
- A book of idioms (see BRAIN CANDY) might help if you can find one, but it's not necessary

Let's Cook!

Think of a well-known book or movie title, for example, *The Polar Express*. Now take one of the words (say, **polar** for this one), and start to think of words that rhyme with it or sound like it. I thought of **molar**.

Now trade out the original word with the new one and you have *The **Molar** Express*. You have just created an answer to a question that has not been asked. All you have to do now is to come up with a question, like *What kind of train takes you to the dentist?*

Drop your new joke on the next unsuspecting person, and when you reveal your answer, be sure to laugh out loud at your own joke, which will make it an official pun.

Take turns seeing who can come up with the worst puns, then share a few of them with family members at the dinner table (*if it's permitted!*).

CHEF'S TIPS *Use a phrase or title most people are familiar with, because otherwise they won't get the pun.*

What cookies do you like best?

Baltimore Oreos!

Baxter Says: Me? Yow!

Puns are fun because, unlike a test at school, you come up with the answer first, then the question. What could be better than that?

Tongue Twister Taffy

Try saying this three times as fast as you can:

Sister Suzy's Selling Thirty Thirsty Thistles.

Can you do it? If you find it a little difficult, join the club. Just like taffy, which is twisted again and again until you can't remember where the start was, tongue twisters often leave their players dizzy and tongue-tied.

Tongue twisters also come in poetry or stanza form (which isn't any easier). Here's a popular one:

Peter Piper picked a peck of pickled peppers;
A peck of pickled peppers Peter Piper picked.
If Peter Piper picked a peck of pickled peppers,
Where's the peck of pickled peppers Peter
   Piper picked?

Ready to tie your tongue in knots? Then let's pull some words!

I am the very model of a modern Major-General,
I've information vegetable, animal, and mineral,
I know the kings of England, and I quote the fights historical
From Marathon to Waterloo, in order categorical;

I'm very well acquainted, too, with matters mathematical,
I understand equations, both the simple and quadratical,
About binomial theorem I'm teeming with a lot o' news,
With many cheerful facts about the square of the hypotenuse.

To get a good feel for the nature of The Pirates of Penzance, recite the two paragraphs above as fast as possible.

Gilbert and Sullivan's opera (Wait! This is good!) *The Pirates of Penzance* is a great way to hear some rapid-fire tongue twisters, also known as *patter*. If you have a chance to hear it sometime, be prepared to listen closely.

Baxter Says: *Me? Yow!*
The faster you play, the sillier it gets!

JAMES JOINS JACKIE'S JOYFUL JOB JAUNT...

appeal: what you get from a banana.

PUNZLES®

Recipe

skill level
MEDIUM
LOW — HIGH

serves: 4 or more players
ingredients:
• A dictionary helps!

Let's Cook!

Have all players sit in a circle. Decide who goes first. The first person starts by saying one word, usually a first name, such as *Frank*. The next person repeats what was said and adds to the tongue twister: *Frank finds*. The next person adds to that, as in *Frank finds forty*, and so on.

Keep going around the circle until someone messes it up. The player who misses starts the next round.

We never kept score on this game, 'cause we were always laughing too hard.

Did we **Baxter** last week?

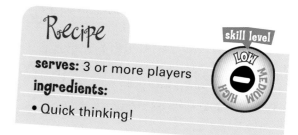

Recipe

skill level

serves: 3 or more players

ingredients:
• Quick thinking!

Baxter Borscht (it's hard to beet!)

*B*orscht (pronounced BOARSH, also spelled *borsch*) is an easy-to-prepare Russian soup that uses beets. It's a very simple meal, and so is BAXTER BORSCHT, which is similar in play to SODA POP SWAP (page 74). In some countries the game is known as Coffeepot or Teakettle.

In BAXTER BORSCHT, the Guesser is asked to identify what *verb* the others are replacing with the word **Baxter**. (You know Verb, don't you? He's the character who makes things happen.

Without Verb, there'd be no action when a movie director shouted "Quiet on the set! Lights, camera, *action!*" He makes you run, jump, play, sleep, think, laugh, sing … and cook! Without Verb, there would be nothing happening. Thank goodness for Verb!)

Let's Cook!

Choose a Guesser and send her out of the room, or have her cover her ears and sing "The Star-Spangled Banner," while the others agree on the hidden verb.

Then let the Guesser come back in and question the others, asking, for instance, *What time of day do you usually **Baxter**?* or *Can my mother **Baxter** in the kitchen?*

The Guesser may ask 10 questions, to which the other players must give sensible answers. If the Guesser thinks of the secret verb by the end of the 10 questions, she receives one point, and another Guesser is chosen.

The first player to reach five points is the winner.

initial ingredients (who will win?)

Here's a simple recipe for fun that involves the main ingredients of wordplay — the alphabet! This cooks up pretty quickly, so you'd better have your brain in high gear.

Let's Cook!

One Leader is chosen from the group. The Leader shouts out the letters of the alphabet in order and the players each try to be the first one to say a word that begins with that letter. The first person to give a correct answer wins one point.

When the alphabet is finished, the person with the most points becomes the next Leader.

CHEF'S TIPS
- *Individual players can keep track of their scores, or the Leader may track it for everyone.*
- *To make the game more interesting, shout the letters of the alphabet out of order (you'll need pencil and paper for this!), or have the players agree on a topic, such as food ("A" "Apple!"; "B" "Banana!") before play begins.*

F!

Pharmacy!

Recipe

skill level

serves: 3 or more players
ingredients:
- Pencil and paper (optional)

LOW MEDIUM HIGH
0

KEYWORD KABOBS

_____

acronyms

cannot: when something won't fit into a can.

Book Bag Barbecue

I packed my bookbag, and in it I put gasoline, french fries, world peace, 12, air, the Detroit Pistons, lasagna, and kryptonite!

Recipe

skill level MEDIUM

serves: 2 or more players

ingredients:
• Good memory

Let's say that your family is driving all the way to Boston to see that darned Red Sox (*Darned Sox.* Get it?) team play baseball. You may not share everyone's enthusiasm for the game, so you'll need something to do for the trip.

Well, now's a good time to mix up some BOOK BAG BARBECUE (traditionally known as I Packed My Bag, or Grandmother's Suitcase). And, just like a real barbecue, you need to keep on your toes, or you'll get burned!

Let's Cook!

The first player begins by saying, *I packed my book bag, and in it I put …*, followed by an item. The next person repeats the phrase but has to add another item. Play continues back and forth until someone forgets an item in the book bag. The game goes on until everyone but the winner has been disqualified.

Items that you pack in your book bag don't need to be normal items, either, which makes the game much more fun. *I packed my book bag, and in it I put … loafers, a pencil, my horse, a 1968 Camaro, a drawing pad, a box of cereal, New Jersey, a gallon of milk, tickets to the next Kansas City Chiefs game, a pickle, an outboard motor …*

See what I mean?

CHEF'S TIPS *Make it more challenging by adding items in alphabetical order, so that each new item has to follow the next letter of the alphabet, as in "I packed my book bag, and in it I put an apple, a brownie, coats, dolls …" Or, make a rule that everything must be related, such as only sporting items, as in "I packed my book bag, and in it I put acrobat rings, a baseball bat, a canoe, my dirt bike …"*

Bizz Buzz Biscuits

So you think you're good with words, eh? How about words and numbers *mixed together*? Actually, to make BIZZ BUZZ BISCUITS you need to remember only two words: **Bizz** and **Buzz**. Remembering *when* to use them is something else, though.

Let's start cooking with just Buzz words, then sprinkle in the Bizz.

Let's Cook!

Start the Buzz: All the players sit in a circle. Going clockwise, begin to count one number per turn. When a player gets to a number that has 7 in it (as in 17, 27, 37 …) or is a *multiple* of 7 (as in 14, 21, 28 …), the player says *Buzz*.

If a player makes a mistake, then he or she is out until the next round. The last player left, making no mistakes, wins the game.

Add the Bizz: To kick it up a notch, play BIZZ BUZZ, which uses the numbers 5 (Bizz) *and* 7 (Buzz). When someone gets to a number that applies to both, such as 35, the player must say *Bizz Buzz!*

CHEF'S TIPS *If you get really good at this game, try reversing directions each time a person says "Bizz" or "Buzz" or "Bizz Buzz"! Be prepared for a great deal of laughter and confusion.*

...16, buzz, 18, 19, 20, buzz, 22, 23, 24, 25, 26, buzz, buzz, 29...

Recipe

serves: 2 to 5 (or more!) players

ingredients:
• Concentration!

skill level

HIGH MEDIUM LOW

Brain Candy

You go **clockwise** in this game. Now, there's an interesting word. So, is the clock wise? Does **counterclockwise** mean "an unwise clock"? Why not just say "going **clock-like**" or "going **un-clock-like**"? See how odd the English language can be?

Baxter Says:

Me? Yow!

Younger kids may have trouble keeping track of numbers and words at the same time, so work with them. Someone probably did the same for you when you were just a wee wordsmith.

Limerick Lasagna

anapestic, clerihew,
Edward Lear, limerick, poetic
meter, rhyme sequence

Unless you've been locked away in a tower that is guarded by an evil wiener dog for several years, you are probably aware that lasagna is made by layering different kinds of food in a casserole dish. Well, limericks adhere to a similar code. They are five-line poems where the first, second, and fifth lines rhyme with and have the same meter (or beat) as one another, and the third and fourth lines, which are shorter, rhyme with and have the same meter as each other.

Here's a classic to get you started:

A flea and a fly in a flue
Were imprisoned, so what could they do?
Said the fly, "Let us flee."
"Let us fly," said the flea.
So they flew through a flaw in the flue.

Limericks are not the easiest poems to invent, so I suggest you enlist the help of some friends. Get out your oven mitts, use your noodle, whip up some LIMERICK LASAGNA, and see if anyone likes the taste.

A puppy and kitty both frowned
'Cause they would be put in a pound.

A home was their aim
And soon they became

The very best pets ever found.

Let's Cook!

Sit with others in a circle, and take turns writing one line of a limerick. Player 1 thinks of the first line, Player 2 must think of a second line that rhymes, then the next player works on the third line, and so on, until a limerick appears.

Write down your final limerick in your Noodle Book, and share it with others. Watch out, though! When friends and family taste your creation, they may tell you that it needs more salt.

Baxter Says:

Me? Yow!

Keep all your phrases sweet.
And gossip? Don't repeat.
'Cuz time and again
(You won't know when)
Those words you *might* just eat.

Brain Candy

If you're interested in more limericks, check out Edward Lear's *A Book of Nonsense* (first published way back in 1846!).

Who tripped and then fell on her noodle...

There was a young girl name of Foodle...

PUNZLES

WIGWAM & TEEPEE
MUSEUM

Word Chain Casserole

Recipe

serves: 3 or more players

ingredients:
- Pencil and paper or Noodle Book (optional)

skill level

LOW MEDIUM HIGH

Word chains are some the easiest things to cook up, and can be prepared very quickly by someone with very little "kitchen" experience.

A *word chain* is a list of words (usually around a specific topic) in which the *last* letter of the previous word is the first letter of the next.

Why are you looking at me that way? Okay, maybe I should give an example.

doG
GoldfisH
HampsteR
RabbiT
TurtlE
English bulldoG
GerbiL

See how it works? The previous words are all types of pets. Now you and your friends can give it a taste.

Let's Cook!

Choose a topic (movies, books, first names of boys or girls, pets, and so on). One person starts with one word, and the play passes to the next person. Each person in the group, in turn, must come up with the next word that fits the chain.

If someone fails to come up with a

word or uses a word that someone else already said in that round, she is out. The winner is the last person still "adding ingredients" to the word chain casserole. Or, you can play that if you can't think of anything that hasn't been said before when it's your turn, you get a letter in **C-H-A-I-N** against you (or **W-O-R-D C-H-A-I-N C-A-S-S-E-R-O-L-E** for a really long game!).

CHEF'S TIPS
- *If you use a two-word name like **New York** or **English bulldog**, use the first letter of the first word and the last letter of the last word for the word chain. The same is true of names of people, unless you are playing last (or first) names only.*
- *Play using pencil and paper, or a Noodle Book, if you want to save the casserole for later (leftovers, anyone?).*

Liar, Liar, Pans on Fire (20 questions with a twist)

Uh-oh! Is something burning in the kitchen of the WORDPLAY CAFÉ? Smells like someone is scorching the *truth* a little bit.

Almost everyone has played the game 20 Questions, especially on long road trips, or perhaps when waiting more than an hour just to see the doctor's assistant! To play, one person thinks of an object, then allows other players 20 questions in which to guess what the object is.

Let's warm things up with a recipe that puts a little extra heat on 20 Questions.

Let's Cook!

Select one person from the group to think of a word or object. The other players have 20 chances (or questions) to uncover what the person is thinking about. Each question must be able to be answered with **yes** or **no**.

KEYWORD KABOBS
guessing games, 20 questions

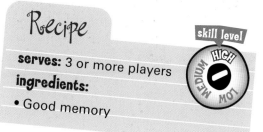

Recipe

skill level

serves: 3 or more players

ingredients:
• Good memory

Is there one in this room?

No!

The fun part to this particular recipe for the game is that the person being questioned always tells the *opposite* of what she means (so *yes* means "no" and vice versa — *no* means "yes"). Only when a player guesses the object correctly does the truth come out.

Be prepared for lots of confusion!

Brain Candy

***Vice versa* is from** the Latin *vice* (or *vicis*), meaning "position," and *vertere*, meaning "to turn." So when you do a vice versa, you change positions!

Baxter Says: Me? Yow!

Is the stove in your kitchen as friendly as mine? Every time I go to use it, every one of the dials has the word **HI** *on it!*

Cooking School Recess

So, you've twisted your tongue, swapped your soda pop, and barbecued your book bag. Are you tired yet? Well, I am. Let's put down the spoons and toss the bowls into the sink for a moment, and have another shot at PUNZLES® play. Just in case you were absent when we did the first one (page 56), I'll go over the rules again.

Highlighted in **RED** in the following story are words that describe items in the image (next page), but instead of being literal clues, they are phonetic puns. As an example, for the word *apparent*, think *"a parent."* See how many words and images you can match. You'll find the answers on page 124.

It was now apparent. Joseph would be able to finish his homework (thank goodness for the spell-check) before his dad would ask his advice on the fine art of cabinetry. He knew that his mother would adore his handiwork, but could not account for his sibling's taste in carpentry. He was no coward, but his entry in the State Fair's box contest would be an honest test of his skill. Joseph thought to himself, "I believe this could be the one!"

The plans (which were laced with woodworking jargon) were laid out on the carpet in his room. "There is no way I'm going to be able to fit this through the door when it's finished," he said, so off he ran to bring some helpers aboard. "Is what we're doing illegal?" asked his brother Jack, who liked spending time in the trees. "You've been watching too much TV," said Joseph. "It's a perfectly acceptable manner of reusing wood."

Except for the occasional bloopers that Joseph had while working on his project, everything seemed to come out okay. There was no way a judge would degrade his project, so a gold medal was as good as in the bag!

Ad Slogan Swap Slop

Gosh, if I could only find some advertising somewhere. I need something with a good slogan, something that everyone has heard. Where, oh where will I find advertising?

How about *everywhere*?! People (kids especially) have never been so over-whelmed by advertising — in magazines, on TV, on the radio, on T-shirts, shoes, caps, blah, blah, blah. There is so much advertising going on these days, I thought it would make for some great wordplay.

Here's the deal: I like to take the first part of an ad slogan (also called a *jingle*) and combine it with the ending of another totally separate product, as in

this mix between M&Ms and Manwich Sloppy Joes:

M&Ms melt in your mouth
... but a Manwich is a meal!

Or, how about this one from Rolaids and the American Beef Council:

How do you spell relief?
It's what's for dinner.

Sound like fun? (At least it sounds *different* — and that's refreshing.) I think if we have to listen to advertising garbage, I mean, uh, slogans, we should get to make fun of them at every turn.

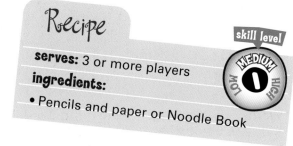

Recipe

skill level **MEDIUM** / LOW / HIGH / **1**

serves: 3 or more players
ingredients:
• Pencils and paper or Noodle Book

Let's Cook!

The next time your friends are over to watch TV, grab some paper (or your Noodle Book) and make notes of adver-tising slogans you hear. (And you will hear *plenty*!)

After you have a few (change the channel if you need some fresh ones), begin to take them apart and stir up some AD SLOGAN SLOP! Remember, sometimes you feel like a nut ...

If You Spilled It, He Will Come. Bob's Carpet Cleaning 4812 Main Street

KEYWORD KABOBS

bait and switch,
false advertising,
jingles, slogans

Do the Ads Have Your Attention?

Words, words, words ... and more words! Kids and adults these days are being bombarded with advertising. And yes, even *I* am guilty of advertising. Look in the back of this book and you will see a list of books that I (and my publisher) hope you'll consider buying.

So, do you buy jeans or video games or action figures or candy because you really want them? Or is it because advertising has made you think that you simply can't live without them?

Of course, advertising has its place. I am very happy with my iPod, for instance, and I'm glad that the Apple company told me about it through commercials. However, if I can ask one thing of each and every one of you, it would be this: **Listen to your *own* advice on how to spend your money, not the advice of someone shouting at you from the TV.**

Taste Test

Take the Ad Challenge. Can you replace the **blank** *in the following phrases with the correct word?*

You deserve a* blank *today.
Just* blank *it.
Betcha can't* blank *just one.

If you can complete even one of these ad slogans correctly (answers on page 124), consider yourself "branded" by the advertising industry. Perhaps a little less TV is in order. Got books?

cement: what you do when you go to see how coins are made.

Baxter Says:

Me? Yow!

My name is Baxter Kline and I approved this message.

Brain Candy

If you really want to "refry" your writing, try using *mirror words* (page 63) on every other line. It may take some time, but you'll like the result, and your code will not be quite so easy to crack!

Jamal, if you can read this letter, better much doing are you then than some of my other friends. .it get to seem don't just They

Refried Reverse Writing (& reading)

Sometimes we take words and to learn we Once .granted for letters read, we tend to forget about the .read just and rules

Notice anything funny about the paragraph above? Let me help. Read the first line. Then, starting on the right-hand side, read the next line of words right to left, then back to normal for the third line, then right to left again for the last line.

This is called *reverse writing*. In school we are taught to read left to right and top to bottom, but many other cultures don't share our rules for writing. Reverse writing is almost like a code, but easily figured out.

chain reaction: what happens when the swing on the playground breaks.

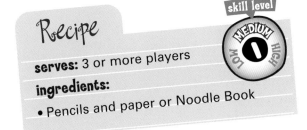

Recipe

serves: 3 or more players

ingredients:
• Pencils and paper or Noodle Book

skill level

LOW MEDIUM HIGH

Let's Cook!

Each player writes a paragraph of at least six lines using reverse writing. Pass the result to the player on the left, and challenge him to read it out loud.

Oxymoron Tail Soup

This isn't really a recipe. It's more of a story about how odd the English language can be. Feel free to make note of these in your Noodle Book, but for the moment, put down the spoon and step away from the bowl!

Oxymorons (not a bunch of stupid cattle) are words used together that contradict each other.

Most oxymorons are simply used to dramatize parts of speech, and we don't even stop to think about what the words themselves really mean. But if you start to listen, some of them are downright ridiculous! They can be found in many places. Here are a few of the more obvious:

- **jumbo shrimp**
- **civil war**
- **pretty ugly**
- **freezer burn**
- **sweet tart**
- **only choice**
- **crash landing**
- **non-stop flight**

Can you think of any oxymorons? If you can, write them down. You might also be surprised to learn that many authors have used oxymorons in their verse, including William Shakespeare, Ogden Nash, Emily Dickinson, and Mark Twain, to name a few.

Pretty ugly

AUTHOR

KEYWORD KABOBS

contradictory, oxymora, oxymoronic

Brain Candy

Did you know that if you are a *sophomore*, you are an oxymoron? The word **sophomore** is likely from the Greek *sophos* ("wise"), and *moros* ("stupid"). Maybe sophomores just aren't sure in which direction to go, just yet.

Reversed Spelling Bee Brownies

How good is your spelling? Do you think that you might qualify for the Scripps National Spelling Bee (see page 24) in Washington, D.C.? Whatever your spelling prowess, I think you'll enjoy playing this game. But wait!

If there's anything you've learned so far at the WORDPLAY CAFÉ, it's that things may not be as simple as they seem.

Let's Cook!

Select one person as the Chooser. That person chooses a word from the dictionary (nothing too difficult) and asks the first player to spell it ... *backward!*

The player must pronounce the word, spell it backward, then pronounce it again. If a player makes a mistake, she is out. Play continues until only one person is left (the winner!), who then becomes the Chooser for round two. Play continues until players can no longer spell because they are laughing too much.

Recipe

serves: 3 or more players

ingredients:
- Pencil and paper
- Dictionary

skill level

KEYWORD KABOBS

cacography, orthography

Acronym.
M-Y-N-O-R-C-A,
Acronym.

Acronym.

parade: when your dad bursts into your room looking for dirty dishes.

PUNZLES®

Dr. Puzzle Will Shortz, Ph.D.

Nearly every Sunday morning since 1987, *The New York Times* Crossword Puzzle editor Will Shortz (and host Liane Hansen) have bewildered, entertained, and otherwise enlightened listeners — and call-in participants — with their brand of word wizardry on *Weekend Edition*, heard on most NPR (National Public Radio) stations.

Having some fun with that?

Okay, here's a bit of trickery to try out on an unsuspecting speller. Ask someone (even an adult!) to recite the alphabet backward. It's pretty hard to do, so your friend, if he takes the challenge, might take a long time stumbling through the letters (Z-Y-X-W-V-U-T, and, so on). When he's done, say "I can do it a lot faster." Then turn your back to him and recite the alphabet the normal way. Gotcha! An even simpler version is to just say the phrase "the alphabet backward" when it's your turn to do the reciting, after your friend fumbles. Double gotcha!

Baxter Says:

Correct spelling is very important, especially if you are filling out a job application or writing a thank-you note. Really! Often, adults who make a spelling mistake on a job application get the "circular file" treatment — the application is tossed in the trash and they are immediately eliminated from the pool of job candidates. It's the first clue to a potential employer as to your "smarts" (or at least to your attention to details). And if you're writing a thank-you note, well, it sure makes a better impression if the words are spelled correctly!

Will is the only person in the world with a college degree in Enigmatology (the study of puzzles), which he earned from Indiana University in 1974.

I strongly encourage you to check local listings (or go to **npr.org** on the Web) and play the *Weekend Edition* Sunday Puzzle along with Will and Liane to see just what kind of wordplay person you are. After all, you can't go wrong when it's delivered right to your door!

Brain Bran with Rotated Reading Relish

My two sons, Steve and Jon, are some of the most avid readers in the family. They simply gobble up book after book, probably because I made reading fun for them when they were little.

I would often adopt a very fake accent when I would read (my favorite was British), or purposely change the names of characters, which my boys would correct immediately!

But one of the most fun things to do involved turning their reading world upside down. Here's the recipe for how to do it.

Let's Cook!

Choose one person as the Chef. Each player attempts to read one page loudly and clearly while the Chef slowly spins the book.

There is a certain book-spin speed at which the reader will still be able to read, although she may get dizzy. Getting it right may take some practice.

After all players have had a chance to read a page, the Chef passes the book to a new Chef, then takes a turn at rotated reading.

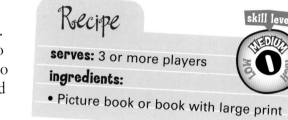

Recipe

skill level

serves: 3 or more players
ingredients:
• Picture book or book with large print

honest: where a mother bird usually sits.

How Do You Really See Words?

Try reading the following paragraph:

Ocne uopn a tmie, trehe lvied in the froest a very lagre ginat who would garb peploe that wakled by.

If what you've just read is a story about a giant that lived in the forest, then congratulations. You're doing fine!

When we learn to read as children, we first learn letters, then words, then phrases, until we can quickly glance at a sentence and grasp its meaning.

A lot of words that we use are identified by their first and last letters, as in the paragraph about the giant. Notice that only the inside letters have been moved around, and that all the letters are there.

We recognize things by their parts all the time.

Say, for instance, you see someone coming toward you at school with glasses, black hair, and a red sweatshirt. You immediately recognize that person as your friend, just by those traits — you don't need to see him up close, or see his freckles, blue eyes, or shoes or socks, to know who it is.

Well, that's the way reading works, too. You begin to recognize familiar words, just like old friends.

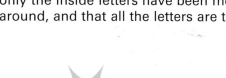

Want to kick it up a notch?
Try rotating the book while holding it up to a mirror, and see if you can still read it. If you can, then you are a very observant reader!

PUNZLES®

Nutty Neologisms

You think I'm making this up, don't you? Well, I'm not beyond a little white lie every now and then, but there actually are words and phrases known as *neologisms* (nee-AH-lah-jizms). And they have a very special place at the WORDPLAY CAFÉ, because ... they're made up! Just my cup of tea.

The official definition of a neologism is "a new word, usage, or expression." It also means (and this probably fits me better) "a meaningless word used by a psychotic," which goes a long way in explaining why I call this NUTTY NEOLOGISMS. At any rate, I've managed to turn it into a game (er, recipe). Are you with me? Perhaps I should give few examples ...

From **homework** and **weekend**

Weapons of grass destruction:
lawnmowers.

Internot (from Internet and not):
when your mom won't let you check
your email.

Homewok (from homework and wok):
a deep, large, round frying pan
that you'd like to toss your math
assignment into.

Are you catching on yet? If you are, then let's cook!

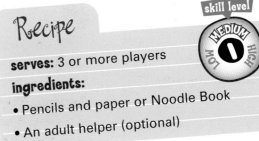

Recipe

skill level

serves: 3 or more players

ingredients:

• Pencils and paper or Noodle Book

• An adult helper (optional)

Tack support:
The people you call when you're having problems using carpet tacks.

Ploystation:
A video game that tricks you.

Arithmetick:
A small parasite that is very good with numbers.

Every month for 21 years, *Washington Post* columnist Bob Levey has asked his readers to come up with their own neologisms. The rules are simple: He provides contestants with an obscure definition, as in "The first child born into most families ends up with a meticulously kept and thorough baby photo book. Siblings that follow never do as well. This phenomenon is called ... ," then asks his readers for the new word (or phrase). The responses for this one included **rugrationing**, **receding heir line**, **Polarvoid**, **scrapped book**, and the winner, **photigue**, from the words **photo** and **fatigue**.

Let's Cook!

Players sit in a circle. Each player thinks up and then writes down one neologism with its definition. Once everyone has finished writing, take turns reciting the neologisms. Then vote on which neologism you think is best. (Or, ask an adult bystander to serve as an impartial Judge.)

Give one point for each win. After five rounds, crown the neologism champ!

Save your neologisms and email them to friends to get their reactions to your "new" words.

CHEF'S TIPS
Neologisms are easy to create. Just think of a word or phrase you use all the time, as in **email**. *Now add, drop, or change a letter or two (it really doesn't matter), and you have, let's say,* **shemail**, *or* **hemail**, *or even* **fleamail**. *Now think up a defintion, as in* **fleamail: email composed with a very, very small typeface**. *See?*

malign: "Don't run with scissors!" is one.

Spoonerisms You Can Eat with a Fork

Have you ever accidentally mixed up your words by switching parts of one word with parts of another? If so, then you already know what a Spoonerism is.

Made famous by the Reverend Archibald Spooner (see BRAIN CANDY, next page), Spoonerisms are often hilarious, as in the following phrases that he unwittingly muttered:

"Mardon me, padam, but you are occupewing the wrong pie. May I sew you to another sheet?"

Spoonerisms can be used on almost anything, as in the following nursery rhyme:

Dumpty Humpty wat on a sall,
Dumpty Humpty grad a hate fall,
All the Hing's korses and all the
  Ming's ken
Pouldn't cut Tumpty hoogether
  again.

Here at the WORDPLAY CAFÉ, we'd rather you whip up a sad ballad than serve a bad salad, so that you can really taste what Spoonerisms are all about!

Look! Isn't that the Dig Bipper?

metathesis, spoonerism, transposition

Baxter Says: Me? Yow!

When you start to move word sounds around, you may accidentally come up with a word that is a no-no, so play it smart!

serves: 3 or more players

ingredients:
- Newspaper
- Pencils and paper or Noodle Book

Let's Cook!

Invite some friends over and dig out the movie section of yesterday's newspaper. Take the titles of current movies and Spoonerize them, making notes on your paper. If you run out of movie titles, check out the TV listings for the names of shows.

Compare your results with the other players to see who comes up with the funniest Spoonerisms. And remember, there is more than one way to Spoonerize!

PUNZLES®

Billion Dollar Maybe!

Squarebob Spongepants!

Around the 8 In Worldy Days!

Loam Ahone!

America's Hunniest Foam Videos

Brain Candy

William Archibald Spooner, whom Spoonerisms were named for, was born in London in 1844 and eventually became an Anglican priest and scholar. Reverend Spooner spent 60 years at Oxford University, where he taught history, philosophy, and divinity. From all accounts, Spooner was said to be one of the original absent-minded professors.

Nifty Swifty Stew (for Toms & Sarahs)

I happen to love Tom Swifties and Sarah Swifties, mostly because the pun comes at the very end of the joke, so the unsuspecting tester of your joke is left with an odd look on her face (until she gets it).

Swifties are sentences in which adverbs (most often) relate to a word or phrase both properly and in a pun, as in the following:

"The door is ajar," said Tom *openly*.
(relates to door)

"I seem to have found some plutonium," said Sarah *glowingly*.
(relates to plutonium)

...Sarah said sheepishly.

...Tom said belatedly.

Sometimes the Swifty is even more of a pun and harder to catch:

"I can't believe that Elvis is dead," said Tom *expressly* (ex-*Presley*, get it?).

See how it works? Then "Sharpen up your knives and let's cook," said Tom bluntly.

KEYWORD KABOBS

wellerism

Recipe

serves: 3 players (but can be played by just 1 or even by 8!)

ingredients:
- Pencil and paper or Noodle Book

skill level
LOW **MEDIUM 0** HIGH

Let's Cook!

Gather up a few close friends, put some popcorn in the microwave, and start to brainstorm on some Tom and Sarah Swifties.

The best way is to think up the punch line first, such as *Sarah said sharply,* then come up with the initial line, such as *"May I please have the scissors?"* Then put the two together.

"Vote to see who can come up with the best Swifty," Tom said democratically. "Reward the champion with a large bowl of popcorn," Sarah suggested winningly.

Tom Swift was an adventurous character invented by writer Edward Stratemeyer (also known as Victor Appleton), who often had Tom qualify a statement with a pun. He was also the guy who master-minded the *Hardy Boys* stories, which you might have heard your parents (or grandparents) talk about, and maybe have read yourself!

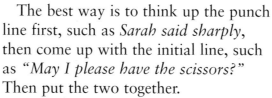

"Mondays are meant for blue jeans," Sarah said casually.

Baxter Says: Me? Yow!

Forgotten what an adverb *is? Remember, it's a word that describes a* verb *(page 80). Many, but not all adverbs have LY at the end, he explained* loudly, *then* quietly *and* quickly, *somewhat nastily, then sweetly ... you got it!*

You-Don't-Say Buffet

Gosh, how should I put this? It's kind of like, well, hmmm. What I want to say is, oh crud! Never mind.

Sometimes the most fun word games come from words that are *not* spoken. Do you suppose it's possible to play word games without words?

I know what you're probably thinking right now. Something like, "This guy has pushed his headphones a little too far into his ears."

Well, fear not, my word-chomping chums, you will know how to play before you can say … YOU-DON'T-SAY BUFFET!

Let's Cook!

Each player is given five "lives." An everyday word is chosen, such as **yes** or **no**, then each player takes turns talking non-stop for two minutes without using the word. If that person messes up, he loses a "life."

Play continues with the same word until all players have had a chance, then a new word is chosen and play begins again. The winner is the player who is still "alive"!

And!

I went to the store, ummm, where I spent twelve dollars on some food, errr… as well as some gas for the car an —oops! Anyway, I drove around the park, while looking at the ducks, ummm…

KEYWORD KABOBS

evitation

Brain Candy

Words such as **yes**, **no**, **this**, and **that** are hard to avoid sometimes, and if you really want to make it difficult, try to not use the words **and** and **I**!

I got Britney an ivefay eedspay illdray and an etpay oabay onstrictorcay.

Pigs-Latin in a Blanket

Oday ouyay inkthay athay eway areway avinghay unfay etyay?

Wrapped in a warm pastry of confusion, Pig Latin is one of the easiest (and most entertaining) languages for kids to speak. All you have to do is remove the first letter (unless it's a vowel) of a word, move it to the end, and add AY. Or, if the word begins with a double letter sound, like "th" or "gr," move both letters to the end. If the word begins with a vowel, simply add the letters WAY or YAY to the end of it.

I always thought it was funny when my parents would talk about Christmas presents using Pig Latin, 'cause I always knew what they were saying. It was a good time for me to play stupid.

So, fire up that oven between your ears, abgray omesay otdogshay, andway et'slay avehay omesay unfay. Allway ouyay eednay isway ouryay imaginationway!

Let's Cook!

Find a favorite book and take turns reading paragraphs from it to one another in Pig Latin. At first it may seem difficult, because you are literally translating a language as you speak.

The more times you do it, the easier it will become. Soon you can become a Pig Latin–speaking foreign correspondent!

Recipe

serves: 3 or more players
ingredients:
- A book and some mental energy

Can you figure out (see art) what Britney is getting for her birthday? To test your skill, check your answers on page 124.

jargon, opish, turkey Irish, Ubbi Dubbi

Baxter Says:

Me? Yow!

Be careful when using a secret language, because the one thing it states very clearly is "I have something to hide." So, all detectives' ears will pick up. Plus, most adults used to speak Pig Latin, too, because kids have been speaking Pig Latin for a long, long time!

Hink-Pink Think Drink

I've just noticed that I haven't wasted a lot of paper on riddles yet. And what kind of place would the WORDPLAY CAFÉ be if there weren't any riddles? Umm, no, that wasn't a riddle.

One of the easiest riddle games to play is called Hink-Pink. You simply find two words (of one syllable each) that rhyme, then devise a question or riddle. Some examples:

What do you call a home for a small rodent? (a _mouse house_)

What do you call a piece of wood where amphibious creatures sit? (a _frog log_)

What is an angry father? (a _mad dad_)

So, get those brain juices flowing with a nice, tall glass of HINK-PINK THINK DRINK.

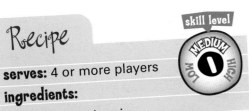

Recipe

skill level

MEDIUM / LOW / HIGH

serves: 4 or more players

ingredients:

- Pink lemonade mix
- Pencils and paper or Noodle Book
- A rhyming dictionary might help, but it's not necessary

Let's Cook!

Make up a pitcher of pink lemonade while your players are gathering their thoughts. Have all players come up with their own Hink-Pinks, then let each player ask a riddle of the rest.

Keep track of who gets the most answers after each round, name that person the "Pink Wizard," and toast her with pink lemonade!

Brain Candy

Hink-Pinks can also be played with two-syllable words (Hinky-Pinky) and three-syllable words (Hinkiddy-Pinkiddy). Award additional points for anyone who comes up with Hinky-Pinkies or Hinkiddy-Pinkiddies.

*kid vid

Chapter 5ive

PC PANCAKES: WORD GAMES WiTH A COMPUTER

TABLE NO.	DINERS	SERVING NO.	005

Okay! Let's go and surf the Web
For lots of pun and games.
We'll translate phrases, words, and more
(Remember, don't use names!)

For typos that occur too much,
A website is the spot!
Relax. Just point your mousie to
This verbal turkey trot.

Blue Plate Special

Computer Cabbage

Computers are wonderful things. Most of my work is done on a computer, allowing me to sit in my home office in Wichita, Kansas, and work with people all over the country.

But like anything else (especially cabbage), if handled incorrectly, computers can really stink things up. So before you begin playing word games on a computer (yours or someone else's), let's review the basic rules for PC play and safe surfing (see "Computing Do's & Don'ts").

Computing Do's & Don'ts

- **Do** — always — ask permission to use someone else's computer.

- **Do** follow the "house rules." If a parent or other adult allows a certain time for you to use a computer, *please stick to it.*

- **Don't** — *ever* — give out your name, address, phone number, school name, or other personal information to anyone you don't know.

- **Never** respond to emails or IMs (instant messages) without consulting an adult.

- **Never** click on links in or open emails from people you don't know (a *virus* — a computer "bug" — may be lurking there!).

- **Do** share your computer games with the family, 'cause we all learn from each other.

On pages 9 and 29, I mentioned that the rules could be bent if you can think of a better way to play. But let me state very clearly, *rules for computer use are not to be bent in any way!*

Does this make me sound like an annoying adult? If it does, remember that you will someday be one, too, and if you care anything about your kids, you will use the same strict language. So now, my wee sidekicks, boot up and get cooking! Season the pot with SALT & PEPPER SEARCH ENGINES (next page), if you like.

Baxter Says: Me? Yow!

If you know of a friend who is viewing improper websites, tell an adult you trust. This is serious business! Telling may save your friend's life!

kingdom: what people say when they think the king isn't very smart.

Salt & Pepper Search Engines (the basics)

Aaa-choo! (Or should I say @*choo*?)

...16, 17, 18...

At one time or another (like throughout this whole book!), you'll likely want to use a search engine to hunt for information on the Internet. A *search engine* is a website or program that looks through a huge database of information and reports the most meaningful results according to your keywords or question.

One word can bring up many search results. Now, if your parents would let you stay on the computer for weeks at a time, going through all those choices would not be a problem. Most of us, however, need to move a little faster. A search engine eases the load.

I'll take you through some of the cooking basics for using a search engine. Spoons and mouse ready?

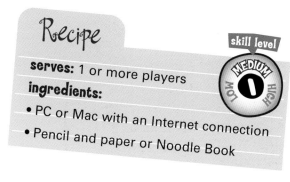

Recipe

skill level

MEDIUM

LOW — HIGH

serves: 1 or more players

ingredients:

• PC or Mac with an Internet connection

• Pencil and paper or Noodle Book

Let's Cook!

Turn on your computer. Go to the search engine that you use most frequently (it has its own World-Wide Web address, such as www.google.com). Some examples are Google, Ask Jeeves, and Yahoo! You can try out different ones to find what works best for you.

Now, what do you want to know? Type in a keyword (like one of the KEYWORD KABOBS throughout this book) or a phrase that seems to sum up what you are looking for, such as **kid's word games.**

How many responses did you get? Do they give information on what you wanted to know more about? If there are too many websites listed, or if they don't really seem to be what you were looking for, type in your keyword or words again, but try to be more specific. See the CHEF'S TIPS, page 110, to help refine your searching.

KEYWORD KABOBS

Boolean searches, web crawler

- *Narrow your choices (enter **michelangelo** rather than **artist**)*
- *Use words that you think will appear on the site (enter **shrek action figure**, not **really cool shrek toy**).*
- *Don't include connecting words such as **in**, **and**, **of**, and **the**. They are too common.*
- *Search for a specific phrase by putting it between quotation marks (**"star wars episode 1"** will return only the sites containing that phrase).*
- *Limit your searches by using special characters, such as a minus sign (**bass** can mean a fish or a guitar, so try **bass –fish**, being sure to leave a space after **bass**).*

Googol **is the mathematical** term for a 1 followed by 100 zeros. The term was coined by Milton Sirotta, nephew of American mathematician Edward Kasner, and was popularized in the book *Mathematics and the Imagination* by Kasner and James Newman.

The Google search engine company's play on the term reflects its mission to organize the immense amount of information available on the Web.

I googled you today, dad!

Enter Internet Ingredients

Perhaps now would be a good time to stop and "sharpen our knives" with a discussion about the Internet and what it's made of.

First, some definitions: The *Internet* is commonly thought of as the connection (at first physical, now often wireless) between everyone's computers. The *World-Wide Web* (better known to you as the www. before website addresses), on the other hand, is the actual collection or database of information available through those connections. Make sense?

Although they serve two distinct functions, we often refer to them as one and the same. So when we use the terms Internet (or the 'net) and the Web, we're really talking about the same thing: huge amounts of information available to many people.

Who, When, Where

Though you, my witty wordsmith, have likely had access to computers all of your life, the technology isn't so far back in the olden days as you may think.

Just a little more than 50 years ago, in his 1945 article "As We May Think," Vannevar Bush imagined people being able to scroll through all human knowledge at a desk-like machine he called a Memex. Then, in 1959, J.C.R. Licklider wrote *Libraries of the Future*, about how a computer could provide an immense network of information (an automated library) that people could access from home.

In 1962 the IPTO (Information Processing Techniques Office) was formed (as an arm of the ARPA or Advanced Research Projects Administration, a group originally created in the name of national defense). By the end of the 1960s — under the direction and work of engineers Bob Taylor and Larry Roberts — two very large computers, one at the University of California in Los Angeles (UCLA) and the other at the Stanford Research Institute, began talking to each other. As early as 1971, computers at various universities and research companies were doing the same. The rest, as they say, is history.

As I'm writing this book, there exist more than 800 million Internet connections worldwide. English is the language of choice on nearly 70 percent of them. Why make so much of the Internet in a book about wordplay? Just try imagining the Internet without words …

How many acronyms can you find on this page? (Answers on page 124.)

ARPAnet, cyberspace, e-commerce, netiquette

Translation Toast

Recipe

skill level

MEDIUM **1** LOW HIGH

serves: 1 or more players (but more fun with 2 or more)

ingredients:
- PC or Mac with an Internet connection
- Translation website or application

Let's make some toast! But for this browned bread, let's run it through the toaster several times and see what happens (no, it won't be burnt toast, I promise!). Are you with me?

There are many websites (and PC-based applications) that offer to translate words from one language to another. This service is one of many great things that computers are very good at. But of course, *I* found a way to play with it.

Take particular note of the following two paragraphs:

When I was a little boy, I played a game called dogfoose, where the rules were always changing, and fun was the goal.

My little boy was in this moment, played my play dog elected load, where the standards always changed, and pretty was an object.

Do both paragraphs seem remotely connected, yet oddly distant? Here's the deal:

I took the first paragraph, translated it into Dutch, then into French, then Spanish, then back to English. So by the time it got back around to English, it was barely recognizable. And I don't think putting jelly or jam on it is going to help, either!

Let's Cook!

Write a short letter (some websites allow only 150 words) or use a familiar poem, and translate it several times. Each time it will probably get further and further from the original. What seems similar and what makes absolutely no sense in its translation? Be sure to use your computer's "copy" and "paste" functions to make things go quicker.

Wood are beautiful, dark and in profundity
But I have the promises to maintain
And the miles outward journey initially that it sleeps
And miles to go initially which sleeps*

*from a popular poem by Robert Frost

KEYWORD KABOBS

babel, etymology, interpret, neologism, tower of Babel, translate

Online Word Game Goulash

There are literally hundreds of word games available on the Internet and as PC applications, even the popular Hangman (see page 37)!

Some of the more popular are tongue twisters, cryptograms, crossword puzzles, hidden words, Text Twist, Bookworm, Flip Words, and Scrabble. Some let you play online, and some will let you purchase (with an adult's permission, of course) and download the game directly to your computer.

Most word games will have you play against the clock, so remember, practice makes perfect!

Recipe

skill level

MEDIUM

serves: 2 or more players

ingredients:
- PC or Mac with an Internet connection
- A quick mouse finger

Let's Cook!

Choose a word game online and share that information with some friends. Each player takes a week or so to master a certain game, and then you all compare your highest scores. (Agree ahead of time how many hours

Guess what? I just scored over 5000 points on Word War II!

Bah! I find your assertion of ascendancy both unmeritorious and self-aggrandizing!

you and your friends will play, so that you have the same practice amounts.)

There's also a good chance that one of your friends will find a better way to play the game and share her tip with you. You can do the same!

KEYWORD KABOBS

online word games

Baxter Says:

Me? Yow!

Sorry, I must repeat here: NEVER BUY SOMETHING ONLINE OR GIVE OUT ANY INFORMATION UNLESS YOU HAVE HELP FROM AN ADULT!

Typo Tea & Biscuits

The coming of the Intrenet (page 110) meant that a lot of people could openly exchange a great deal of infromation with others, and that information could change rather quickly.

The Internet is considered to be *dynamic*, or always changing. Other mediums such as books and photografs are considered *static*, or not changing.

Recipe

serves: 1 or more players

ingredients:

- PC or Mac with an Internet conection
- A good set of eyes

skill level MEDIUM 1 LOW HIGH

And guess what? Because the Internet is available to almost anyone, it is a breeding ground for mispelled words! Here at the WORDPLAY CAFÉ, we sometimes misspell words on purpose, but the World-Wide Web is no place for bad spelling (typos). The reason for people to use correct spelling when creating Web pages is simple: It allows people to locate your site using keywords!

PUNZLES® answer: Microchip.

Let's Cook!

The next time you visit a website, see how many spelling mistakes or typos you can find. With an adult's permission, perhaps you could even send an email to that website and let the Web master know that some words are misspelled. Chances are, he may not even be aware of the mistake, and may appreciate your attention to detail.

Taste Test

I've purposely misspelled 16 words on pages 114 and 115 (and made one up). Can you find them all? (Answers on page 124.)

Baxter Says:

Me? Yow!

Websites aren't the only places you can find typos. What about your own work? Whenever you are writing something on the computer — say, a letter or a report for school — print out a copy and proofread it carefully before you turn it in. Errors seem to be overlooked when you read on the screen, but they are easier to spot on a paper copy.

Brain Candy

When I would send emails to art directors of magazines asking them to use my artwork, I would type the word **jected** into the subject line. When they would reply with a note saying, "Your work is not what we are looking for at the moment," the subject line would read **RE:jected**. Go into the dictionary and look under the words that start with RE. Do you see any ideas for your emails?

...25, 26, 27, 28, 29, 30, 31, 32...

Pun-Hunting Punch

I love puns and punning (page 76), especially when my pun-inflicted listeners roll their eyes and groan. When I witness such a reaction, I think, "Bingo!" Other people besides me must like puns, too, because my latest search for the word **pun** on the Internet gave me 1,640,000 results! How do I view this overwhelming mountain of data? As a gold mine!

The Web is a great place to find puns, if for only one reason: Often, seeing one pun will make you think of another. So if you're looking for some new material, have your Noodle Book handy, and dive into that big punch bowl of information we call the World-Wide Web.

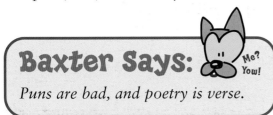

Baxter Says:

Puns are bad, and poetry is verse.

Let's Cook!

Use a *search engine* (see page 109) such as Google or Ask Jeeves to hunt for puns.

!Caution! *When you dive into a website that contains puns, don't dive in too deep without checking for approval. Some puns contain (yikes!) not-so-nice four-letter words!*

KEYWORD KABOBS

equivoque, Richard Lederer, paronomasia, punning, puns

Chapter Sicks

PUT WORDS TO WORK iN YOUR KiTCHEN

TABLE NO.	DINERS	SERVING NO.	006

Mnemonics are a great way to
Remember all those things,
Like pi and why to multiply,
And even names of Kings.

So Alpha Bravo Charlie to
A friend (it's code, you see).
Make friends with a *Thesaurus rex*,
And take a break (like me!)

Blue Plate Special

Mnemonic Nutrition

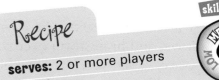

Recipe

skill level

serves: 2 or more players

ingredients:
- Pencils and paper or Noodle Book

If you were asked to prepare a dessert (like chocolate pudding) in the desert (such as the Sahara), could you do it? Or better yet, how could you tell one from the other? Easy.

The sweetest one has two sugars!

Huh? Is the author of this book one sandwich short of a picnic?

That may be true, but what I'm getting at is a clever use of _mnemonics_, or memory devices. Most mnemonics use words, as in the case of **dessert** vs. **desert**, in which the sweetest (the dessert) has **two sugars** (meaning **two S's**).

Here are a couple that students of music use all the time: **E**very **G**ood **B**oy **D**oes **F**ine (the notes represented by the lines — bottom to top — on the treble clef), and **FACE** (the notes represented by the spaces between the lines, bottom to top).

Mnemonics find favor, especially with kids or kid-minded adults (like me!), because phrases are easier to remember than long lists. They also come in handy when trying to recall math formulas (as in _my_ case).

What? That's easy! Just remember:
Old Henry
Always Has
Old Apples.*

mnemonics

*Used in trigonometry to remember the equations for Sine (Opposite over Hypotenuse), Cosine (Adjacent over Hypotenuse), and Tangent (Opposite over Adjacent).

Let's Cook!

Plop down on a floor somewhere with lots of pillows, and brainstorm over some list or set of rules that you have trouble remembering. Then come up with your own mnemonics to help you recall them with ease!

If even one good mnemonic results from your brainstorming, then everyone wins!

Baxter Says:

If someone requests the value of pi, just ask, "May I have a large container of coffee, Madam?" The number of letters in each word is the value of pi to the 8th place (3.14159265).

How about this? Super Mitch Hurries Early On.*

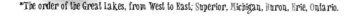

*The order of the Great Lakes, from West to East: Superior, Michigan, Huron, Erie, Ontario.

Brain Candy

Mnemonics (ni-MON-iks)? Who thought of *that* crazy spelling? They are named for Mnemosyne, a goddess of memory in Greek mythology. She and her husband Zeus were the parents of the nine *muses* (Calliope, Clio, Euterpe, Thalia, Melpomene, Terpsichore, Erato, Polyhymnia, and Urania), whose collective talents lend themselves to the word **museum**. Perhaps Mnemosyne needed a way to remember the names of her children ...

Taste Test

See how many of these mnemonics you can decipher. Then check your answers on page 124.

1. *Richard Of York Gave Battle In Vain.*
2. *Kids Prefer Cheese Over Fried Green Spinach.*
3. *Red Right Returning*
4. *Spring ahead, Fall back.*
5. *Camels Often Sit Down Carefully; Perhaps Their Joints Creak? Persistent Early Oiling Might Prevent Permanent Rheumatism (this one's tough!)*
6. *My Very Educated Mother Just Served Us Nine Pizzas.*

Phonetic Alphabet Soup

Recipe

skill level

serves: 1 or more players

ingredients:
- Email (or paper and pencil, envelope, and stamp)

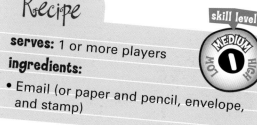

otel Echo Lima Lima Oscar! Hotel Oscar Whiskey Alpha Romeo Echo Yankee Oscar Uniform Delta Oscar India November Golf?

By now you're probably thinking, "Michael Kline must not be the sharpest knife in the drawer." But fear not, my phonetic friends, I've just said, "Hello! How are you doing?" using a device called the *phonetic alphabet* (also called the IPA, or International Phonetic Alphabet), which uses code words to identify letters in voice communication.

You've probably used it, or heard it used, without even knowing it existed. When people talk on the phone and use initials (as when you want to register a video game or computer, or get a confirmation number for an order for a cool pair of Nikes or a plane ticket to some exotic island), it's often hard to distinguish between B's and C's, G's and D's,

because they can all sound alike. So instead of trying to super-clearly pronounce a G, you can just say "Golf."

I've written out the IPA so you can learn it for yourself. It's especially useful in radio communication by aircraft personnel, amateur radio operators, and people in the military.

Let's Cook!

Compose an email (or snail mail) to a friend using the phonetic alphabet. Make it simple, at least for the first time. You might need to let the recipient of the letter know about this kind of alphabet, as she may wonder if you lost all of your Mike Alpha Romeo Bravo Lima Echo Sierra!

This is Whiskey Oscar November Delta Echo Romeo Foxtrot Uniform Lima!

KEYWORD KABOBS

futhark, international phonetic alphabet, NATO phonetic alphabet, phonotype, visible speech

Taste Test

Can you decipher the two codes on this page? (Answers on page 124.)

Brain Candy

Phonetic Alphabet

A	**Alpha**	(AL-fah)
B	**Bravo**	(BRAH-VOH)
C	**Charlie**	(CHAR-lee)
D	**Delta**	(DELL-tah)
E	**Echo**	(ECK-oh)
F	**Foxtrot**	(FOKS-trot)
G	**Golf**	(GOLF)
H	**Hotel**	(hoh-TELL)
I	**India**	(IN-dee-ah)
J	**Juliett**	(JEW-lee-ETT)
K	**Kilo**	(KEY-loh)
L	**Lima**	(LEE-mah)
M	**Mike**	(MIKE)
N	**November**	(no-VEM-ber)
O	**Oscar**	(OSS-cah)
P	**Papa**	(pah-PAH)
Q	**Quebec**	(keh-BECK)
R	**Romeo**	(ROW-me-oh)
S	**Sierra**	(see-AIR-rah)
T	**Tango**	(TANG-go)
U	**Uniform**	(YOU-nee-form)
V	**Victor**	(VIK-tah)
W	**Whiskey**	(WISS-key)
X	**X-Ray**	(ECKS-RAY)
Y	**Yankee**	(YANG-key)
Z	**Zulu**	(ZOO-loo)

Whip Up Your Imagination!

Have you ever used electric beaters to whip heavy cream into a delectable topping for chocolate pudding, pumpkin pie, or hot chocolate? Or beaten egg whites into frothy peaks for meringue cookies or key lime pie? Whipping adds lots of air and transforms boring old cream or egg whites into an entirely new, foamy, taste experience.

Your imagination is kind of like that, too. If you don't whip it (use it much), it isn't very, well, *imaginative*. But if you give it lots of air and make it churn around, it becomes an incredible, amazing tool that you can use to do all sorts of things you never imagined before!

There I was, stranded on a couch that was bobbing up and down in a sea of green shag carpet. My only hope was to somehow make it to the coffee table where, if I was lucky, I could leap to the lounge chair, then out the door to the relative safety of linoleum. All would have gone well, but upon entering the kitchen, I suddenly remembered that my parents were actually robots being piloted by tiny aliens, seated at the controls behind the eyes of both Mom and Dad. "They'll not have me this time!" I vowed, and sped off for my bedroom closet that I had recently converted into a dual-purpose time machine and communications center.

Has Michael Kline forgotten to pay his brain bill? Perhaps. But what's really at work here is my imagination. The story you just read is from my distant (yet very clear) past.

The 1956 Thunderbird Spaceship

When I was a kid (some of my publishers think that I still am), I had a wild imagination. The green 1956 Thunderbird parked in the backyard was my own personal means of planetary transportation, complete with milk-carton breathing devices, coffee-can gauges, and flashlight lasers.

We didn't have trees in the backyard, only gnarly, wooden legs of huge creatures that had long since been buried upside down, leaving only their lower limbs exposed aboveground. (If I clambered around in them just right, it would tickle the creatures back to life — which my mom said was only the wind. But I knew better. *Ha!*)

What about *your* imagination? Is it asleep or awake? Does it visit you sometimes when you don't want it to, as, say, at church or school? Well, imagination can be a hard thing to control, but we all have one. We use it everyday, especially when we need to be creative, when we have a problem to solve, or when a typical answer to a question just won't do. And that's just what the WORDPLAY CAFÉ is all about: imagination.

Take an Imagination Break!

When you need to have that spark of creativity, do yourself a favor. Get some blankets and clothespins, and make a tent in the living room (with your alien's — oops, I meant *parent's* permission), or grab a flashlight laser and head for the nearest closet (I mean, *time machine*), and create your own adventure.

Stand on your head (use a pillow, it's much more comfortable) in the rec room and imagine what it would be like to walk around on the ceiling! Try drawing a picture of your favorite pet — with your eyes closed!

Try seeing things in a new way. Use your imagination to see words and the world around you differently. Once you learn how to put that imagination to use, you'll find that wordplay is as easy as whipping up egg whites!

Roger, Victor. I have just passed the gas giant Dogfoose 5!

Thesauri, Dictionaries, Idioms, Word Origin Books, Slang Dictionaries & Other Word Cookbooks

Every time I go into a bookstore (which is often), I trace a familiar path.

First, I head to the kid's section to see *what's hot*. I find the sections on science for kids of particular interest (as do some other adults — maybe the simpler explanations are easier for them, too!), after which I head straight for …

THE REFERENCE SECTION (yes, I'm a party animal)! I just love looking through the books that explain how words work, and tell about different languages, idioms, word origins (did you know that the word **pinkie** is from the Dutch word *pink*, short for *pinkje*, meaning "small"?) — in short, everything to do with words!

There are many types of reference books that deal with words and languages, so if you're interested, visit the library (take your Noodle Book!) or local bookstore, and begin your own treasure hunt for wordplay. To get you going on your quest, check out some of my suggestions at right.

dictionary, etymology,
homophones, idiom,
lexicography, onomasticon,
slang, thesaurus, word origins

THESAURUS REX

A Dictionary of Homophones by Leslie Presson (Hauppage, N.Y.: Barron's Educational Series, Inc., 1997)

The Dictionary of Wordplay by Dave Morice (available from the Teachers & Writers Collaborative, 5 Union Square West, New York, NY 10003-3306)

The Facts on File Encyclopedia of Word and Phrase Origins (revised & updated edition), by Robert Hendrickson (Checkmark Books, 2000)

Idiom Savant: Slang As It Is Slung, The colorful lingo of American subcultures, from animators to Zine readers by Jerry Dunn (Henry Holt & Company, 1997)

NTC's American Idioms Dictionary (3rd edition) by Richard A. Spears, Ph.D. (McGraw-Hill, 2000)

Pun and Games: Jokes, Riddles, Rhymes, Daffynitions, Tairy Fales, and More Wordplay for Kids by Richard Lederer (Chicago Review Press, 1996)

Ant Sirs

Words: A Brief History (page 13): *antediluvian* means "ancient."

Slanguage Slaw (page 18): The two portmanteaus are **ebonics** (**ebon**y + phon**ics**) and **slanguage** (**slan**g + lan**guage**).

Taste Test on Quayleisms (page 26): There are many answers for the problems in these funny quotations of Dan Quayle's. Here are a few:

- A "recovery" is what will happen when the president leads us out of a *decline* or a *recession*.
- The line should read "that area of the *world*." Latin America is not an area of a "country," and it certainly is not an area of the U.S.!
- Chicago is a city, not a "state."
- Phoenix is in Arizona, not "California."
- If an "event" is "unforeseen," you have no idea what it may be, so how can you know whether you are prepared for it or not? And if something never occurs, as in "any unforeseen event that may or may not occur," then it is not an "unforeseen event'; it is not an "event" at all!
- Awkward at best, but the biggest blooper here is that what is meant is that we will never surrender to what is *wrong*, not "surrender to what is right."
- A low voter turnout means fewer people went to the polls to vote. That's a fact, not an indication. The fact that fewer people voted could be an indication, however, that there is voter apathy or disinterest in what is going on politically.
- A better way to say the first part might be to say: "If you give a person a fish, he will *eat* for a day." See page 5 for a better paraphrasing of this expression. What is meant is that if you give someone a handout, it helps for only a short period of time. But if you *teach a person a skill*, so that she can improve her daily existence, it will have an effect on her whole life.
- The line would make more sense if it read "the best-educated people in the world." The idea is that the goal is to improve the education of Americans so that they are at the top of the class to compete with the rest of the world.
- Pollution can be defined as, among other things, "impurities in our air and water."

Add a Gram of Anagrams (page 31): The anagram for DORMITORY is DIRTY ROOM.

Palindrome Potluck (page 33): The Taste Test poem has two palindromes, a single word (**deed**) and the phrase **never odd or even**.

Homonym Grits (pages 42-43): A search for incorrect homonyms *in just the text* might turn up: **knight** (night), **End** (and), **awl** (all), **threw** (through), **Knot** (Not), **Knot** (Not), **yew** (you), **sum** (some), **yore** (your), **yule** (you'll), **their** (there), **mini** (many), **yews** (use), **awn** (on), **bases** (basis), **hoarse** (horse). Now you figure out the homonyms in the art!

Verbal Tea (page 44): IBQQZ CJSUIEBZ UP ZPV = **Happy Birthday to You** if you move each code letter one step backward in the alphabet.

Crepes of Wrath (page 54):
neurotransmitter (9): euro, rot, transmit, ran, mitt, it, an, a, I
mathematics (12): mat, math, hem, the, them, a, at, tic, tics, ma, thematic, I
beforehand (12): be, before, for, fore, forehand, hand, or, ore, ha, a, an, and
copyrightable (9): a, I, cop, copy, right, able, rig, tab, table
unintelligible (4): I, in, tell, gib
reallocation (6): I, a, real, all, cat, on
extraterrestrial (11): I, a, extra, at, rate, err, rest, trial, rat, ate, rater

Get Out of the Kitchen (pages 56-57): Big Punzles®
American = a merry can; **amateur** = am mature (the elderly person); **catsup** = cat's up (as the one on the roof); **escape** = S cape (as in what Superman is wearing); **quality** = koala tea; **serial killer** = cereal killer (the milk, which is next to the koala tea); **gigantic** = gigantic tick; **apparel** = a peril (the hole with the Danger sign); **mushroom** = mush room (where dogs train for the Iditarod sled race); **forehead** = 4 head (head implying the outdoor bathroom marked with the number 4); **keyboard** = key bored (as the one in the door); **philosopher** = Phil, officer; **letterhead** = letter head (as in the outdoor bathroom marked M).

Synonym Rolls (page 59): You know this rhyme better as
Hey, diddle, diddle,
The cat and the fiddle,
The cow jumped over the moon;
The little dog laughed
To see such sport,
And the dish ran away with the spoon.

Taste Test (page 59): *The Potentate of the Metallic Circular Enclosures* stands for *The Lord of the Rings*! And the movie *A Succession of Calamitous Circumstances* in the art is better known as *A Series of Unfortunate Events*.

License PL8 Pie (page 62): ICU812 (I see you ate one, too); IRIGHTI (Right between the eyes); 10SNE1 (Tennis, anyone?); AV8R (Aviator); CUL8ER (See you later). And in the art: MOVE-IT

Portrait Pickles (page 66): The W in Williamson Books is part of the company logo.

Zeugma Zest (page 69): In the sentence *With a little practice, maybe you'll get smarter and invited to more parties!*, the word **get** is applied to both **smarter** and **invited to more parties**, for some funny reading.

Soda Pop Swap (page 74): The homonyms in Baxter's poem are **nose/knows**, **sense/scents**, **maid/made**, and **wood/would**.

Cooking School Recess (pages 88-89): Big Punzles®
apparent = a parent (as the one in the car); **spell-check** = spell Czech (which the boy in the car is doing); **adore** = a door (there's one on the house, one on the car, duh); **account** = a count (as in Dracula); **coward** = cow word (moo); **entry** = in tree (as in the boy and both birds actually); **box** = bawks; **honest** = on nest (one of the birds is); **believe** = bee leave (which is what happened when...); **jargon** = jar gone (or broken, so the bee

leaves!); **carpet** = car pet (the dog); **aboard** = a board (which the man is carrying); **illegal** = ill eagle; **bloopers** = blue purse; **no way** = no weigh (which is the out-of-order scale); **degrade** = D grade (which I received on some of my test papers too!)

Do the Ads Have Your Attention? (page 91):
You deserve a **break** today. (McDonald's)
Just **do** it. (Nike)
Betcha can't **eat** just one. (Lay's potato chips)

Pigs-Latin in a Blanket (page 105): Britney is getting a five speed drill and a pet boa constrictor for her irthdaybay.

Enter Internet Ingredients (page 111): The acronyms are **IPTO** (Information Processing Techniques Office), **ARPA** (Advanced Research Projects Administration), **UCLA** (University of California in Los Angeles).

Typo Tea & Biscuits (pages 114-115): **Intrenet** (Internet), **infromation** (information), **photografs** (photographs), **mispelled** (misspelled), **conection** (connection) are misspelled in the text; **jected** is the made-up word; and in the art, **kars** (cars), **prises** (prices), **freindly** (friendly), **srevice** (service), **wekends** (weekends), **moduls** (models), **stok** (stock), **hole** (whole), **yuor** (your), **rebaet** (rebate), and **avalable** (available).

Mnemonic Nutrition (page 119):
Richard Of York Gave Battle In Vain. Order of colors in the rainbow, or visual spectrum: Red, Orange, Yellow, Green, Blue, Indigo, Violet

Kids Prefer Cheese Over Fried Green Spinach. Order of taxonomy in biology: Kingdom, Phylum, Class, Order, Family, Genus, Species

Red Right Returning. A nautical mnemonic to help boats navigate safely. Boats **returning** to a harbor from a lake or the sea pass **red** buoys to the **right** (starboard) side of the boat (thus **red right returning**) and the green markers stay to the left.

Spring ahead, Fall back. When and how to adjust your clocks for Daylight Savings Time and Standard Time (set clocks ahead by an hour in spring, set them back by an hour in the fall).

Camels Often Sit Down Carefully; Perhaps Their Joints Creak? Persistent Early Oiling Might Prevent Permanent Rheumatism. The first letter of each word is the first letter of the geological time periods, oldest to the present: Cambrian, Ordovician, Silurian, Devonian, Carboniferous, Permian, Triassic, Jurassic, Cretaceous, Paleocene, Eocene, Oligocene, Miocene, Pliocene, Pleistocene, and Recent.

My Very Educated Mother Just Served Us Nine Pizzas. The first letter of each word gives you the first letter of the planets, in order: Mercury, Venus, Earth, Mars, Jupiter, Saturn, Uranus, Neptune, Pluto.

Phonetic Alphabet Soup (page 120): MARBLES (in the last line of text); WONDERFUL! (in the art).

Still stumped? Email baxter@dogfoose.com for more help.

N Decks

N Decks (continued)

More Good Books from Williamson Books

Williamson Books are available from your book-seller or directly from Williamson Books. Please see the last page for ordering information or to visit our website. Thank you.

All books listed are suitable for children ages 7 through 14, and are 128 to 160 pages, 11 x 8 1/2, $12.95, and fully illustrated, unless otherwise noted.

IN THE DAYS OF DINOSAURS
A Rhyming Romp Through Dino History
by Howard Temperley, illustrated by Michael Kline
64 pages, 8 1/2 x 11, $9.95, full color

Parents' Choice Approved
GREAT GAMES!
Old & New, Indoor/Outdoor, Travel, Board,
  Ball & Word
by Sam Taggar; illustrated by Michael Kline

KIDS WRITE!
Fantasy & Sci Fi, Mystery, Autobiography,
  Adventure & More!
by Rebecca Olien; illustrated by Michael Kline

USING COLOR IN YOUR ART!
Choosing Colors for Impact & Pizzazz
by Sandi Henry

Parents' Choice Recommended
KIDS' Easy-to-Create WILDLIFE HABITATS
For Small Spaces in City, Suburbs, Countryside
by Emily Stetson

Parents' Choice Honor Award
Skipping Stones Ecology & Nature Award
MONARCH MAGIC!
Butterfly Activities & Nature Discoveries
by Lynn M. Rosenblatt
96 pages, 100 full-color photos, 8 x 10, $12.95

Parents' Choice Recommended
Children's Digest Health Education Award
The Kids' Guide to FIRST AID
All About Bruises, Burns, Stings, Sprains &
  Other Ouches
by Karen Buhler Gale, R.N.

HANDS AROUND THE WORLD
365 Creative Ways to Build Cultural Awareness &
  Global Respect
by Susan Milord

Parents' Choice Recommended
THE KIDS' BOOK OF WEATHER FORECASTING
Build a Weather Station, "Read" the Sky & Make
  Predictions!
by meteorologist Mark Breen and Kathleen Friestad

KIDS MAKE MAGIC!
The Complete Guide to Becoming an Amazing
  Magician
by Ron Burgess

Parents' Choice Honor Award
American Institute of Physics Science Writing Award
GIZMOS & GADGETS
Creating Science Contraptions That Work
  (& Knowing Why)
by Jill Frankel Hauser

Selection of Book-of-the-Month; Scholastic
  Book Clubs
KIDS COOK!
Fabulous Food for the Whole Family
by Sarah Williamson and Zachary Williamson

Parents' Choice Gold Award
American Bookseller Pick of the Lists
THE KIDS' MULTICULTURAL ART BOOK
Art & Craft Experiences from Around the World
by Alexandra Michaels Terzian

American Bookseller Pick of the Lists
Parents' Choice Approved
SUMMER FUN!
60 Activities for a Kid-Perfect Summer
by Susan Williamson

THE MYSTERIOUS SECRET LIFE OF MATH
Uncover How (& Why) Numbers Survived from the
  Cave Dwellers to Us
by Ann McCallum, full color

GARDEN FUN!
Indoors & Out; In Pots & Small Spots
by Vicky Congdon, 8 1/2 x 11, 64 pages, $8.95

40 KNOTS TO KNOW
Hitches, Loops, Bends & Bindings
by Emily Stetson, 8 1/2 x 11, 64 pages, $8.95

Parents' Choice Approved
BAKE THE BEST-EVER COOKIES!
by Sarah A. Williamson, 8 1/2 x 11, 64 pages, $8.95

Dr. Toy 100 Best Children's Products
Dr. Toy 10 Best Socially Responsible Products
MAKE YOUR OWN BIRDHOUSES & FEEDERS
by Robyn Haus, 8 1/2 x 11, 64 pages, $8.95

KIDS' EASY BIKE CARE
Tune-Ups, Tools & Quick Fixes
by Steve Cole, 8 1/2 x 11, 64 pages, $8.95

ForeWord Magazine Book of the Year Finalist
DRAWING HORSES
(that look *real!*)
by Don Mayne, 8 1/2 x 11, 64 pages, $8.95

KIDS' EASY KNITTING PROJECTS
by Peg Blanchette, 8 1/2 x 11, 64 pages, $8.95

Parents' Choice Gold Award
Benjamin Franklin Best Juvenile Nonfiction Award
KIDS MAKE MUSIC!
Clapping and Tapping from Bach to Rock
by Avery Hart and Paul Mantell

Parents' Choice Recommended
Orbus Pictus Award for Outstanding Nonfiction
KIDS' ART WORKS!
Creating with Color, Design, Texture & More
by Sandi Henry

More Good Books from Williamson Books
(continued)

Visit Our Website!

To see what's new at Williamson and learn more about specific books, visit our website at:

www.williamsonbooks.com

(This website has books from Williamson Books and Ideals Children's Publications.)

To Order Books:

You'll find Williamson Books wherever high-quality children's books are sold or order directly from Williamson Books, an imprint of Ideals Publications:

Toll-free phone orders with credit cards:
1-800-586-2572

We accept Visa and MasterCard
(please include the number and expiration date).

Or, send a check with your order to:

Williamson Books
Orders
535 Metroplex Drive, Suite 250
Nashville, TN 37211

Please add **$4.00** for postage for one book plus **$1.00** for each additional book. Satisfaction is guaranteed or full refund without questions or quibbles.

Ally Cat

I f you didn't know it by now, Baxter is a real cat, and he came from an animal shelter. Pound puppies and pound kitties make great lifelong companions. There is probably an animal shelter or Humane Society in your town. So if you're looking for a wonderful pet (you may even find one like Baxter), contact your local animal shelter or point your Web browser to www.pets911.com for more information on how and where to adopt a friend in your neighborhood. Remember, pets need you just as much as you need them.